PENGUIN BOOKS

JERUSALEM

Colin Thubron was born in London in 1939. His earliest travel books were about the Middle East and include *Mirror to Damascus* and *Jerusalem*. In the last of the Brezhnev years he explored Western Russia by car and wrote *Among the Russians*. Later, a gruelling journey took him to some of the remotest regions of China for his *Behind the Wall*, which won the Hawthornden Prize and the Thomas Cook Travel Award. Eight years later Thubron wrote *The Lost Heart of Asia*, which describes his travels through Central Asia. He is also the author of a number of highly praised novels, including *Emperor*, *A Cruel Madness* (Silver Pen Award, 1985), *Falling* and *Turning Back the Sun*. Many of his books are published by Penguin.

JERUSALEM

COLIN THUBRON

PENGUIN BOOKS

PENGUIN BOOKS

Published by the Penguin Group
Penguin Books Ltd, 27 Wrights Lane, London W8 5TZ, England
Penguin Books USA Inc., 375 Hudson Street, New York, New York 10014, USA
Penguin Books Australia Ltd, Ringwood, Victoria, Australia
Penguin Books Canada Ltd, 10 Alcorn Avenue, Toronto, Ontario, Canada M4V 3B2
Penguin Books (NZ) Ltd, 182–190 Wairau Road, Auckland 10, New Zealand

Penguin Books Ltd, Registered Offices: Harmondsworth, Middlesex, England

First published in the United States of America by Little, Brown and Company 1969
This edition without illustrations published in Penguin Books 1996
1 3 5 7 9 10 8 6 4 2

Filmset by Datix International Limited, Bungay, Suffolk
Printed in England by Clays Ltd., St Ives plc
Filmset in 10/12 pt Monophoto Bembo

For Charlotte

Acknowledgements

I am grateful to many for help and criticism, but especially to Père H.-M. Couäsnon, OP; Père P. Benoit, OP; Aref el Aref; and Rabbi Dr Philip.

Above all my warm thanks go to the Polish Sisters of St Elizabeth, to Dr Basil Hennessy, Director of the British School of Archaeology in Jerusalem, and to Mrs Rae Jeffs.

Biblical quotes have generally been taken from the Authorised Version; but other translations have occasionally been used.

Contents

I

The Concept

. . . that shadow of a city, Jerusalem.
(ST AUGUSTINE, *The City of God*)

Among the oldest visions of man none is more persistent than the hope of returning one day to a half-remembered innocence. In loneliness he reaches back through emblems – an ikon, a statue or a city – seeking in them a new avenue to God, a fragment of his lost divinity. It was Blake who gave the name 'Jerusalem' to all that was tender and generous in the human soul, writing of her as a woman or as a kingdom whose true spirit fell asleep at the decline of man. For Jerusalem on earth, almost as long as history could remember, had nourished the ideal of holiness, and its betrayal; and like all true symbols she startled an echo in the human subconscious and became herself the Eden which was lost, the imagined time.

Through lands and centuries far from one another, this cadence is twined into the music of religion. In earliest years, it is true, the Jews saw heaven as the dwelling place only of God. They would never share in His dominion, but would pass to *Sheol*, the subterranean republic where the dead lay mindless and unrewarded for ever. Yet already in the wisdom of Isaiah the kingdom of God was prophesied for the cities of men. In Jerusalem, capital of a world at peace, would reign a king to whom all would turn for light. 'Joy of yours, pride of yours, this new creation shall be: joy of mine, pride of mine, Jerusalem and her folk created anew' (Isaiah 65:18, 19). Soon after the return from Babylon, perhaps because there had seemed to be no justice on earth, the Israelites began to envisage a heaven for themselves also. There the city was built again, called *Yerushalayim shel Ma'alah*, 'the Jerusalem of the Upper World', and when their high priest sacrificed to God in the Temple on earth, the archangel Michael followed him through the Temple of heaven.

Long after their dispersal, the Jews looked back in yearning to their fathers' city, radiant with the beauty of the unattainable, and thought it the shadow of paradise. The voice of affection was never lost. 'Ten measures of beauty alighted upon earth,' wrote a medieval sage; 'nine were possessed by Jerusalem, and the tenth was shared by the rest of the world.' Her dust was holy and her people wise, her women lovely, her air pure. At the last day the Temple would rise again upon her rock, and the city would overspread the world with towers and gardens. Seven walls would surround her: a wall of silver and a wall of gold, of precious stones and lazulite, sapphire and emerald and a wall of fire, and all people would come to pray within them, carried on the clouds of heaven.

The concept would have died there, the myth of a scattered race, had the character of the Jews been different; but they took their vision with them wherever they went, and Christianity, inheriting their thought, rebuilt the New Jerusalem in the dream of St John on Patmos, and in St Augustine's belief that Christians on earth were members already of the City of God. St Paul described a free 'Jerusalem in the world above, which is the mother of us all', and Tertullian in the second century AD wrote that 'it is evident from the testimony of even heathen witnesses that in Judea there was a city suspended in the sky early every morning for forty days. As the day advanced, the entire figure of the walls would wane gradually, and sometimes it would vanish instantly.'

Through the Dark Ages men remembered *Urbs Jerusalem beata*, a city whose earthly counterpart they scarcely knew. Crusaders were prepared to die for her, as well as for mercenary causes, and while the medieval centuries praised her in hymn as the Golden and Happy, as the heavenly city moving like a bride to earth, her Moslem captors called her *El-Kuds*, the Holy, and believed that the prophet Mahomet had risen from her ruined Temple on his night journey to heaven.

In the fuller light of the Renaissance the fury to reconquer the earthly city waned, but the trust, the promise of completeness, lingered like a toy in an adult's room, shyly cherished; and Blake touched an old hope when he conjured the fallen spirit from her sleep:

> Awake, and overspread all Nations as in Ancient Time.
> For lo! the Night of Death is past, the Eternal Day
> Appears upon our hills . . .

Yet how could such visions be answered, or a small, misgoverned city hold any breath of lost sublimity? Its prophets were dead twenty-five centuries before – apocalyptic men, not always easy to believe – the promises too long in their fulfilment. There is no alchemy in stones, no miracle on earth. A man may only interpret their meanings, like shadows where they seem to fall, finding God or history according to the balance of his mind. Pilgrims, gathering their indulgences in the holy sites, felt for Jerusalem as had the ancient Hebrews. The city was not built with hands. The imagined lay close above the material and drenched it in the mists and hues of faith. But to Jerusalem today, if he is wise, the religious man carries his dream lightly. Here he is most vulnerable, where his ideals are still enslaved in stone, and if he goes to meet the city as a friend he may find a stranger.

There is a happy tradition that travellers stand on the Mount of Olives before entering the gates. The city shines before them walled and secret, an emanation of the stricken hills. The valleys round her heave and flicker out of the dazzling air; and terraces shored up against the sag of earth and time still hold their musky trees along the slopes. To the south the Judean hills run in blind humps against each other, jostling to Bethlehem. Flaxen villages appear with minarets and pines, and from high up the Dead Sea may be seen shining metallically where the scarps descend unsoftening four thousand feet to the mist of the Moab hills.

A chill settles on the visions of romance and bible illustration. This is the landscape of a harsher holiness, where beauty seems trivial and knowledge is only of God; and after it is watched a while it gains acceptance, like a face remembered. At some diluvian time the land around the city was eroded by violent waters which split her spur with valleys – Kidron, Tyropoeon, Gehenna – and centuries before David the Jebusites built their ramparts savagely above the spoor of the river, fixing the town for trade and self-defence.

It is a haggard site, like any other in this land, and it bore a true daughter to Judea, impassioned, ascetic and cruel. The lines of her early ridges are almost smothered, the small summits and valleys swollen or levelled with the huge waste of daily living and past destruction. The present is gossamer above it. Only in the south-east angle of the walls may one sense how deep the city lies, where the blocks of Herod – blond, enormous and beautifully cut – begin their long thrust through the earth.

The land is always changing, and only the very strong remains. A few years ago, when the barriers still stood between the Old City and Israel, the Mount of Olives was quieter. Now the Jews search for the graves of their families in the wrecked cemeteries and weep on finding them, while Arabs lay their wreaths under the ramparts among the massed tombs of those who died in the last war.

The history of Jerusalem is tragic because people fight for what is precious to them, their allegiance born of another battle, slower and more absolute: the striving of man for God. This other struggle is Jerusalem's peculiar significance, and the radiance of the vision, in any religious life, may lend majesty even to failure. She came to transcend the ordinary laws of towns, her greatness independent of trade. In the saddle of her hills she took business as it came, and added imperceptibly the fine and dangerous commerce of beliefs. By whitened tracks, the roads to Samaria and the coast, her God was carried to the world. She became to the spirit as Athens to the mind; Christianity and Islam were her half-children, and all later elements – Zionism, Arab nationalism, the influence of the West – lie upon a past so pervasive that it forms and guides their growth at every point.

This dream of the divine, strong yet not easily found in its proper purity, is the genius of the city still. Half-hidden in her history and in her people, the essence is there to seek – a tradition spun through many tones and depths, which I could feel only lightly in a single spring and summer: a parable perhaps revealing more of man than of God, but without which Jerusalem has lost her meaning.

2

The City of Law

For in the division of the nations of the
whole earth he set a ruler over every people; but Israel is the
Lord's portion: whom, being his firstborn, he nourisheth with discipline,
and giving him the light of his love doth not forsake him.
(Ecclesiasticus 17:14, 15)

I settled in a foundation of the Polish Sisters of St Elizabeth, who keep a tiny hospice in the soul of the Christian quarter. A year before it had been a part of Jordan, but it was now in Israeli hands and was not yet accustomed. During all the months I stayed scarcely another pilgrim joined us. We lived behind the silence of thick walls, where the alleys climb by steps up the invisible slopes of Mount Akra, and two donkeys may scarcely pass each other. The stone is coral-coloured underfoot and enters the hospice courtyard where the sisters plant infant lemon trees, and forms the floor of all the cells. These are cold in winter, no more than eight feet square, and the chant of the muezzins woke me at a fading hour of night. The stars glitter close in the pure Judean sky. I could imagine myself living in a village, so few are the lights which shine before daybreak. Then a mist rises beyond Moab, and one by one the darkness releases its colours. The east begins to shimmer, to blush out of the roots of its hills, until the sun, nervous and tender in its first shining, touches the crumpled crest of Olivet.

The nuns had grown familiar with this view. Its holiness lay artlessly upon them. It had rained over Galilee, they said, or a sister had gone to Bethlehem, but they were no longer conscious of the radiance in their words. It was the happiness of the convent that little ever happened. The sisters – there were three of them – were pleasantly static, for they felt that they lived at the centre of the world. They were shy and kind, with faces of uncomplicated quiet. But as if to make up for lack of events, the Mother Superior, whom I came to know as La Grande, treated everything as a matter of sudden urgency and dreadful import. Her presence filled the courtyard. She alighted, beaming and effervescent, on invisible problems. She organized and overthrew. Her gestures quickened to a maelstrom and her cheeks quivered when she spoke, even to say 'It's a warm day' or 'Did you sleep well?'

Of the three sisters, one was for a long time too embarrassed to speak to me, but remained closed in upon herself, suffused in smiles and sometimes talking softly to nobody. Another was young, with the withdrawn, oval facc of a High Renaissance madonna; she bobbed and bowed at my approach, as owls do, and it was a week before she spoke to me. She was surprised that I should stay with them, she admitted. There was another Polish hospice in the New Town. It was beautiful, with hot water, and housed a Jewish family and an Arab student, a whole community. She spoke as of a New Jerusalem. Our hospice was for old men, she said, spilling the tea she was carrying, and suddenly pretty in her embarrassment.

But it was an old nun who looked after me: Gentle Sister with water-grey eyes. At first she seemed afraid, and when she opened her mouth only distant sounds came out, like the squeaking of mice behind panels. But later she grew bolder, talking in a voice of plaintive purity, and she anticipated everything I needed.

I had imagined convents to be oppressive, clouded with the vapours of things never said; but as the months passed, these sisters, by the generosity and harmony in their lives, became more than a sanctuary from heat and uproar. Theirs was a standard of religious excellence, which I carried with me like a talisman, remembering it when some trivia made me angry at the monkish world.

It seems absurd to take these qualities for granted, or to expect the ordinary failings to have mysteriously vanished from the hearts of the religious. They are, after all, a microcosm of a cloistered humanity, of history itself as it flows through an ancient and complex city; history which respects nothing so fragile as goodness; the rhythm of an unfeeling universe before which all belief is an act of faith, a step into the dark.

True faith, it could be claimed, began when man first flung in the face of the world his trust in a moral Being, when the tyrant gods fell silent and he saw a justice greater than his own. This first vision, so far as history tells, emerged complete among the Jews, mysterious as a new star; it gave the living force to three millennia, and its city was Jerusalem.

For centuries a comfortable oblivion has settled on the hill of Ophel, except where excavations have exposed the rock, or erosion torn the soft, black earth with veins. Houses and terraces lie over it, but the Ottoman walls, following the sunken lines of nearly two millennia, have cut it away to the south. The Kidron valley falls steeply between hills, and leaves the Christian cemeteries in a wide glade along its withered bed. Sages of all three religions told that those who lie buried here would be close to God on the Day of Judgment. Moslem sepulchres are in the city's shadow, and low on the eastern hill, called by the Arabs 'the Belly of the Wind', the Jewish tombs are almost rained away, and covered lightly with a cloth of grass.

Ophel is pointed southward down the river, the last extension of the city's eastern ridge, and at its point the Tyropoeon valley meets the Kidron, leaving the hill defended on all sides but the north. It is not known when men first came to live there, but some Paleolithic tribe left its traces scattered all around Jerusalem. Already, about 1900 BC, the Egyptians recorded a place named 'Urusalim', which perhaps meant 'City of Peace' or 'City of Salem'; and after Abraham had routed an alliance of local rulers the priest-king of Salem came from the town in fear or gratitude, and greeted him with bread and wine.

Centuries before the Israelites moved up from Egypt, Semitic people sank a shaft to fountain waters at the foot of Ophel. The Bible calls them 'Jebusites', whose 'nativity is of the land of Canaan; thy father was an Amorite, and thy mother an Hittite' (Ezekiel 16:3), and where they piled their stones uncut above the river, the rough angle of a tower remains.

For two hundred years the Israelites fought these people, faded in history, and the Canaanite towns around them. They must have been ugly cities, squat and dense on their arid slopes, and their people joined the Philistines, who came with iron from across the sea, and forced the scattered Jews to unite or be destroyed.

In the last years of the eleventh century BC Saul became ruler in Israel, and died on his sword under the shafts of Philistine archers;

and David, says the Book of Samuel, was anointed king in Hebron, and taught his people the use of the bow. A shepherd from Bethlehem, he became for Israel the ideal of kingship – statesman, warrior and poet. But the house of Saul died only slowly; Jerusalem lay hostile at the waist of the kingdom where an ancient trade route spanned the Judean hills, and you may still pass your hand across the walls, giant and secure on the bedrock of Ophel, and remember the arrogance of the city, whose people called down to David that their blind and lame were sufficient to defend it.

Often the nomads plucked out these strongpoints with their bronze weapons and chariots, not by numbers or ferocity but through native resource. David did not attack the walls but sent a force of men up Jerusalem's water-funnel, one of the *sinnor* common among the Canaanites, for close within the walls the Jebusites had dug a winding passage and dropped a shaft to the fountain pool below. Here in war, when they dared not leave their ramparts for the spring, they lowered buckets through the darkness and drew up the mountain-cooled waters unseen.

'And David said on that day, Whosoever getteth up the gutter, and smiteth the Jebusites, and the lame and the blind, that are hated of David's soul, he shall be chief and captain' (II Samuel 5:8). And Joab, his nephew, adds the Book of Chronicles, 'went first up, and was chief'.

Had he not done so, and the city remained hostile, the kingdom of Israel, divided, might have quietly died, its spirit diffused into the paganism round it; the Law of Moses would have been lost, and Christianity unknown by the form in which it came. But anyone who enters the fountain today and wades for a few yards along its course through the rock, may see a barrel of darkness above him in the torch-light, savage and practical like all things Jebusite, and thrust his toes against the clammy ledges where the soldiers of David crept upward to the light.

Jerusalem became not only the city of Israel's king but the temple of her God, and like Olympia or the Vatican she rested, in theory, above the secular world, a lonely rock in the sea of tribal faction. 'Jerusalem is built as a city', sang the psalmist, 'that is at unity in itself. For thither the tribes go up, even the tribes of the Lord, to testify unto Israel, to give thanks unto the name of the Lord' (Psalm

122:3, 4). The Ark of the Covenant was carried there to the sound of harps and cymbals, and David danced before it, and gave Jerusalem her golden age.

So God was brought with music into the city. He was, it is true, often wrathful and jealous, but these were signs that He cared about the world of men. In His Ark He held a new covenant, the statutes given to Moses on Sinai. His laws were rigid and plain: 'Thou shalt . . .', 'Thou shalt not . . .' It was the code for a young nation, but it fixed absolutely the reality of the good, and by fulfilling its requirements a people for the first time could aspire to a relationship of dignity with God. The Canaanite pantheon – magical, bloodstained divinities of sky and harvest – was drawn by man from a world he could not understand, but the Israelite god rose out of the world within man, and his consciousness of the nation he loved, and was a national and moral Being of a new kind.

The City of David rested in the earlier walls and its houses fell down years later with the terraces beneath them. A few shards moaned faintly wherever I walked, but precisely whose they were may only be guessed. The summit was quarried in Roman and Byzantine times, and where its southern tip lay bare I saw how maimed it was, even the rock-cut cisterns seared away.

Yet there is a lightness and mystery on it. The ghosts of paths and doorways brush the stone. Tombs thrust into the hill, unfamiliar, long and rounded like railway tunnels. Who walked and was buried here, nobody knows. But for centuries only kings could be interred within the city and it was recorded as each ruler died – David, Solomon, Rehoboam – that he 'slept with his fathers and was buried in the City of David'. By the time of Hezekiah there was no room in the royal necropolis, for 'they buried him in the ascent of the sepulchres of the sons of David' (II Chronicles 32:33), and the kings after him were privately entombed. Nehemiah indicates that the royal graves were here on the southern spur, but the shafts were littered now with the refuse of goats.

In David's reign Jerusalem was humble, the city of a shepherd-king, but before his death he gathered materials for the building of a temple to the One God, and bought the threshing-floor of Araunah the Jebusite which stood above Ophel, as he was commanded in a vision. On this windy rock, called Mount Moriah, he raised the altar around which Solomon built the great Temple, and it became in tradition the foundation-stone of the world. Here Adam was created from a spoonful of dust, and returned on his flight from Eden 'to till the earth whence he was taken' (Genesis 3:23). Cain slew Abel upon it, Noah made sacrifice, and Abraham offered Isaac to God. Now the Dome of the Rock, one of the loveliest sanctuaries in Islam, crowns the plateau of the vanished Temple, sheltering the hill-crest which the Moslems call the Stone of Paradise. It is rude and old with worship. Its gashes are too blurred to be deciphered, but it is pierced for an altar lifted to the wind, and may once have been the threshing-floor which David bought with golden shekels for the Temple of his son.

The shrine of Solomon was small, less than thirty-five yards long, but fronted by a porch which glittered golden and stood so high that it could be seen from all the city. No other building has so impressed itself upon the soul of a nation. Half-settled tribes, knowing no luxury but hill-citadels with boulder palisades and plaster floors, saw their Temple rise beneath the hands of Phoenician craftsmen, who jointed limestone walls as smooth as ice, and handled gold as if it were a god.

So carefully was it ordered that the pieces were cut or forged in other places, and assembled later on the hill so that no harsh sounds were heard. Two golden pillars framed its doors, their capitals twined in ornamental fruit and chains, and twelve sculptured oxen shouldered a bowl of brass by the great altar. In the holy hall, feebly lit through high, inviolate windows, floors and ceilings from the woods of Lebanon were covered in a wash of muted gold, and the walls inwrought with cherubim and palms, which glimmered in undying candlelight. Only the Holy of Holies lay in the dark, deep beyond the Temple veil, which the High Priest might enter alone once a year. There the Ark stood and two cherubim touched their golden wings. No god stood in its night, only the tablets of the Law: morality, for the first time, overawing the fetish for an idol.

Nothing is left of this beauty, no block, no chip of sculpture; but it is thought that the stones were hewn in the 'Quarries of Solomon', dug through Jerusalem's northern scarp.

'Solomon hacked out all this,' swore the wizened guard at the entrance. 'It goes on and on. Underground tunnels everywhere. You could lose the Russian army in there!'

He took me down by caverns stained with water, where new blocks had been left half-cut in the walls. The dazzling whiteness of which earlier travellers spoke had gone – the 'Caves of Cotton', silken to the touch, now soiled to common colours. Shale was everywhere, and dust. Here and there the workers left the rock in piers, upholding their stone sky, and blood-red openings gaped suddenly, feverish and fungus-covered, as if struck into some soft, pale mammal.

'Freemasons used to meet here,' the old man said – we had entered a round grotto like a senate. 'Solomon, you know, was their founder; or so they say. But nobody comes now.'

The caves spread on, immense and warm, like the palace of some prehistoric king, gouged by giant arms shaping elemental pillars and poking aborted tunnels with his fingers. The old man imagined cornices and flights of steps and declared that in Roman times the place had been a church.

'Columns and doors, I swear it. *Haida shi bi 'ajjib!* The signs of it are everywhere.' He pulled me aside to passageways where the light bulbs, slung in lonely lines from the ceiling, petered out. The drip of a spring sounded far away. We stumbled along other slashed halls, an endless geometry of stone.

'Steps!' he hissed. 'Pillars!'

He moved my torchbeam over the frescos of the water on the walls, and it seemed as if a rampart stood around us, its pilasters folding one upon the other, like a fan outstretched to darkness.

Deep in all directions these caverns go. From the vast emptiness a city must have come, temples and palaces out of gaps and fissures; but whose city is unknown. We walked its spectral dark and touched the friendly rock, but nothing told the year of its mutilation, or where it went. When we stood far away it seemed clear-cut as a building, but as we came closer it slid to formlessness, and when we talked, the inner caverns murmured in their sleep.

I ascended unhappily to the light, as if some secret had eluded me.

On Ophel only a few ashlars and a broken capital are remnants, perhaps, from the time of Solomon. He ascended a peaceful throne while the Philistines were broken and Assyria slept, but he died ingloriously and the Egyptians took the riches of Jerusalem without resistance. The Philistines returned with nomad hordes to plunder, and the northern tribes of Israel after them; and Ahaz, pressed by old enemies, tried to exchange the gold of the Temple for the aid of the Assyrians, but they could not save him.

Of these centuries I could see scarcely a stone, only clamber for a few feet along a grey scarp, touching with one hand the brute Jebusite tower, and with the other the wall which followed it more than seven centuries before Christ, formidable and integrated still, but many times rebuilt. In this glade of rock and shadow a thousand years go soft-footed to darkness: Assyria rose, Isaiah prophesied, and Canaanite and Hittite princes, long before, passed in a forgotten pageant on the throne which David took from them.

A little to the north is the remnant of a cave-shrine nearly thirty centuries old. It lies under the lip of the holy city – a heathen temple where stones were set up as cult symbols, echoes from the curse of prophets. But the city's life-blood – the Gihon Fountain at the bottom of the hill – still runs in a clear pool. Here Solomon was anointed king to forestall his brother, and rode down on David's mule as a symbol of royalty, with the palace mercenaries around him. 'And Zadok the priest and Nathan the prophet have anointed him king in Gihon: and they are come up from thence rejoicing, so that the city rang again' (I Kings 1:45).

A dragon, said the Arabs, lived covertly beneath the waters and drank them, so that when it slept the level suddenly rose; but the flow is placid now. The local people call it 'the Spring of the Mother of Steps', for a stairway descends through the rocks, beneath which the water rises translucent to the surface of a pool.

A man waded out from darkness and stood watching me, his enormous thighs dwindling to white shadows beneath the surface. For a while he said nothing, but grinned out from the deep like a genial river-monster, dangling his hairy arms against the water.

Then, as if he had been expecting me, he shouted: 'I will show you the tunnel of the king.'

He splashed his arms. '. . . king . . . king . . . king', moaned the cavern.

'King Hezekiah cut a passage through this hill to lead away the river,' he shouted again. 'A great man, very hard-working.'

'. . . -king . . . -king . . . -king.'

He lit a candle and handed it to me across the water. Then, as I stood hesitant, he turned and waded away, climbed some steps unseen beneath the pool, and vanished through a door in the rock, momentarily showing a pair of vast and hirsute legs beneath his knee-length pants.

I took off my shoes and followed him, the water cold above my knees, and passed into another cave, where the pebbles underfoot were rough, and the ice-grey daylight dimmed away.

'And when Hezekiah saw that Sennacherib was come', says the Book of Chronicles, 'and that he was purposed to fight against Jerusalem, he took counsel with his princes and his mighty men to stop the waters of the fountains which were without the city . . . So there was gathered much people together; who stopped all the fountains, and the brook that ran through the midst of the land, saying, Why should the kings of Assyria come, and find much water?'(II Chronicles 32:2–4)

The tunnel wandered ruggedly and passed the silted cave where the Jebusites hacked upward to their city. Then it grew intent with a clean motion through the rock, its floor smooth, and the chisel marks of the king's workmen showed long and white and serried on the stone. As I turned a corner I glimpsed the glow of the man's candle far ahead, lost between the walls and the dark river, and soon I saw him, walking into blackness like a shadow against his own flame, which cast a soft pall on the level rock.

The water ran unnoticeably with us. The way was regular and smooth, a little broader than the men who worked it and no higher than they might raise their arms. The air pressed close where I went in silence, following the light as it faintly glowed upon the surface of the water. Once the ceiling fell so low that it scraped against my head, but often it soared out of reach, where condensation glittered like silver dust, or fell in shining sheaths along the walls.

'Listen,' said the man, and stopped. The rustle of the water round us died; but I became conscious of other noises, irretrievably distant, emanations of the rock and river. I could not tell if they were in my ears or from the air, so pale were they, like songs without voices.

'Every noise travels,' he muttered. 'What you hear could be someone on the hill above. Or maybe in the tunnel far away. I don't know. But the noises gave Hezekiah a bad time. You see how the tunnel keeps changing direction? He didn't know where he was going, but burrowed left and right like a drunken mouse.'

The man was sure that Hezekiah had cut the channel personally: the king had set his little lamp in various niches, and sometimes he had become bored and tried a new direction. And it was true that sockets for the workmen's lights showed as shallow triangles in the walls, and harder rock had bent the tunnel's course. Under the shadow of the Assyrian advance in about 700 BC, two gangs had hacked from each side of the hill, groping towards one another and deflecting strongly, so that the tunnel forms a huge S-bend. But at its centre each party heard the noise of the other's picks through the soft rock, and I saw where they had become momentarily lost, making blind-passes at the walls, before they turned excitedly to meet.

Near the end of the tunnel a Hebrew inscription, now in the Istanbul Museum, was once carved on the side of the wall: 'Behold the Excavation! . . . While the workmen were still lifting up the pick, each towards his comrade . . . a voice was heard of a man calling his fellow, since there was a split in the rock on the right hand and on the left. And on the day of the excavation the workmen struck, each toward his neighbour, pick against pick, and the water flowed from the spring to the pool for twelve hundred cubits, and a hundred cubits was the height of the rock above the head of the workmen.'

We had walked more than quarter of a mile through the hill when I heard voices far away. A seam of light spread over the water, as if people were approaching, and we emerged in sun at the Pool of Siloam.

Aged and quiet, it lies in a bowl of walls where mellow steps descend and the columns of a Byzantine church have left their bases green under the water. Its movement is too gentle to be seen – the waters of Siloam which go softly' (Isaiah 8:6) – and it must have kept this quietness always.

Hezekiah, it appears, covered the pool with a vault then guided the overflow into secret channels, trimming the pink-veined cliffs hard under the southern slopes of Ophel, where the waters still purl. The Assyrians were wasted by plague while they laid siege to the city, and Sennacherib led them back to Nineveh, where his sons slew him.

Seven hundred years later, Christ sent the man born blind to wash his eyes at Siloam, and lepers came to bathe in Byzantine years when a church was spread with porticoes above the water. Even now the Arabs call it the Spring of Consolation, which mends the hearts of those who drink, for its waters, they say, flow underground from paradise.

'But it doesn't work,' groaned my companion, who had materialized from the half-ghost of the tunnel into a substantial and doltish-looking youth. 'Look at my eye. What can water do for that?' A film covered his pupil. He swivelled it blindly at me as we sat by the pool where Christ had granted sight, and held his head in his hands and cursed himself, the water weaving down his legs.

'All my friends call me One-Eye. They say I am no good.' He rocked miserably, still soaked in water like a hippocampus. Then the words rippled out from him in self-intoxicated tides: he was called Jamil; his father, he said, had been killed in the last war with Israel, leaving five brothers and a sister for him to keep. 'If my brothers say "How can we eat?", what can I answer them? Sometimes, believe me, I cry in my bed. I should like to die. But if I die, what will they do? I tried to get a job as a driver, but with an eye like this they wouldn't take me. There may still be a bomb-splinter in here somewhere, believe me.' He pulled down its lower lid and bent towards me, as if asking me to remove a speck of dust. 'Do you see anything, anything at all?'

I couldn't.

'Perhaps there is nothing there. Maybe the bomb fell out of it again. I don't remember anything. I was standing with my father on the terrace of our house, that's all. There was a Jordanian machine-gun post behind us. Suddenly everything blew up. The Israelis were firing huge guns. We never even saw them. All the stones in the valley came up and hit me. Later I woke up and saw. Then slowly the eye went dim. People were all shadows. I lay there for days. I daren't even think about it. Some *tabib* came from the city, but he couldn't do anything. And now look at me: ugly, *ugly*.'

He shivered and slowly pulled on a bleached pair of trousers. 'And I wanted to marry.'

We went back over the Kidron and climbed to the village of Siloam, his village, built among caves and desecrated tombs. If, he added cautiously, he could come by just three English pounds, he could put them down as a deposit and have an operation. But how, he asked, could he possibly find such a sum? He cast his bovine gaze on me, the good eye and the bad eye enquiring together.

I made him work for it. Hc showed me every tomb and grotto on the hillside, wheezing and mumbling as we went: immemorial places scooped from the eroded limestone where Jews had lain buried before the Roman conquest. Byzantine hermits lived there afterwards, and monks came in Crusader years, scratching their Christian symbols on the rock. The slope was enfiladed like a sponge. The ceilings were black with nomads' winter fires, the walls broken in where bugloss hung from shallow cracks and tordylion and buttercups flashed under the pouring sun.

Jamil led me to a low door in the hill, but would not enter. The Arabs hate darkness. When I crawled through, a crypt spread around me, pierced with shafts where skeletons nestled in their dust, and a goat had fallen in and died unfound. The Bible calls this hill the Mount of Corruption or the Mount of Offence, for Solomon, in a degenerate old age, built temples here to please his seven hundred foreign wives, and may have buried his Egyptian consort in the Theban-style 'Tomb of Pharaoh's Daughter', carved from the western slope.

Jamil lived on the summit in a two-roomed house where his little brothers wandered in dreamy shoals. His mother was still pretty at an age when Arab women wither, and might have been a girl but for her lowered breasts. The long, dark dress of Palestine hung beautifully on her, and in the fields she wore the white head-veil fine and unconcealing.

The walls of the rooms were threaded with holes, and Jamil told me what each bullet had done, as if he had watched it. He conjured explosions with his arms, pointing to the house's ruined terrace, and by its fretted windows he recreated pistol-shots in crescendo growls.

'But believe me, now that I have met you I have great luck.

Everything comes from God. Now that you have promised me four English pounds . . .'

'Three.'

'. . . three English pounds, I will be able to see properly and to do everything. Look at my sister, how thin she is. Sometimes I cry . . .'

His sister stared at us through a bullet-hole in the wall – a tiny, simian girl with thick black lashes. 'I'm a lizard,' she said.

There was nothing to cover these gaps in the room except two pictures. One was a Koranic inscription, 'If any man help another, God will support him and give him health', which appeared to be aimed at me. The other was the photograph of a well-known Arab statesman, but Jamil proclaimed: 'That is my father! My heart breaks to look at him! Sometimes at night I think that he is lying in that bed beside me, that he has never gone. Believe me, I could cry to think of his children starving. But now he will be glad for us. We will be able to eat, and I shall drive a lorry, or even a bus. And I shall marry! I have seen a certain girl in our village, and believe me, her breasts are like melons . . .'

He handed me mint tea, the little cup almost obscured in his enormous hand, then fell into a reverie whose figments danced in his eyes: well-fed brothers, a plump, dowried sister, an immense lorry or even a bus, and a prodigally breasted wife. He declared that he would write a letter to the English nation saying how good I was, but to whom this epistle was addressed I never discovered.

Whenever I returned to Ophel I found Jamil grinning to himself and talking about his operation. But one day he vanished, and when I enquired about him from a group of old men, they laughed. Some mad foreigner, they said, must have given him some money. He had gone away. His eye had been ophthalmic almost from birth, and the war had not touched him. 'That house was always rather broken down,' observed one. 'And as for his father, old Mustafa – may God preserve him! – he died peacefully years back.'

Those who had suffered most from the war, I discovered, were slow to talk of it. But Jamil reappeared in a few days and shambled after me all round the Mount of Offence, attempting to justify his lies while I tried to be angry. Wherever he went he cast up huge trails of dust, because his feet dragged, and after a long time he cried for me to stop and shook the stones out of his shoes.

'Believe me, I had *two* fathers . . . My mother, you see . . .'

Far beneath his home the valley gnawed its way south, easing into greenness where the King's Garden, fertile in ancient times, still spread its fig trees round the waters of Siloam. Ophel ends here and the Tyropoeon valley slides into the Kidron, spanned by a dyke of crumbled stones, older than Rome. This, perhaps, was the upper pool where Isaiah preached the coming of a Saviour, but it has been dry for centuries, and already in March it lay under a snow of apple blossom. Nearby Isaiah was swallowed by a mulberry tree while fleeing from his enemies, and a few years ago the friendly trunk used to be shown to travellers.

Here the Kidron is sharp and sunken, and the Vale of Ge-Hinnom moves greyly from the west to meet it until they droop southward as one: used, unhappy valleys with pitted cliffs and evil memories. Ain-Rogel, the Well of Job, is at their confluence under a grass-sown vault, and was given to the people of Jerusalem, they say, for their kindness to Job, who created it by stamping his foot on the rock. Adonijah's followers gathered there to proclaim him king, where the boundaries of Benjamin and Judah met at 'the end of the mountain that lieth before the valley of the son of Hinnom'; and centuries later, runs a Hebrew tradition, Jeremiah descended into the well to hide the holy fire of the ravaged Temple.

The Valley of Hinnom became empty as I ascended, and a hailstorm blew over the Mount of Evil Counsel which darkens it in the south. The barbed wire of the Israel–Jordan frontier still seemed drawn across invisibly. The ancients said that the glade was cursed. Children had been sacrificed there in the fire of Moloch, whose image was bull-headed and filled with flames, its arms extended for offerings, and drums were beaten in the valley to drown the screams of the dying.

'Therefore, behold, the days come, saith the Lord, that it shall no more be called Tophet, nor the valley of the son of Hinnom, but the valley of slaughter, for they shall bury in Tophet, till there be no place. And the carcases of this people shall be meat for the fowls of heaven, and for the beasts of the earth; and none shall fright them away' (Jeremiah 7:32, 33).

After the reign of Manasseh, who sacrificed his own son, Josiah destroyed all that he could; but a curse still lay on the valley, and never died. In Christ's time it was used for the city's refuse, so that a stench and pall of smoke smothered it, and at night the unsleeping fires flickered from end to end of its haunted body. The name Ge-Hinnom contracted to 'Gehenna', and on the Mount of Evil Counsel, it was rumoured, Judas had plotted the death of Christ.

By medieval times the valley had fallen silent. Christian holy men lived in emptied tombs along its rim, and the vale was used for orchards and was covered at last with the dark innocence of earth. But it is said that the holy men were slain mistakenly and buried in their caves, and the whole southern hillside is riddled with sepulchres still. These have been used many times, and some have borders lightly cut in a Hellenistic style, and many more go back to Hebrew years. The whole western slope is a cliff-necropolis, where the dust of pilgrims is scattered through interconnected shafts and chambers.

There is a Greek convent, dedicated to the Egyptian hermit St Onuphrius, who is carved on its gateway with a prodigious and beautiful beard. I walked to it through the lightness of olive trees – clover and pink cranesbill shy on the floor of Gehenna. Nobody answered when I knocked. The iron door was barred. Rubbish heaped about the walls, and I could see the grass grown tall inside and doors swung open against balconies. Somewhere the wind touched a bell. And like a madness of nature the hail came like shot silk from the sky violently, and misted the valley away.

I stood under the arch of Onuphrius, without protection, looking into nothing where Gehenna had been before. The flowers were limp near my feet, and the Field of Blood was crushed in whiteness – the traditional pasture which the elders had purchased with Judas' betrayal-money, thirty pieces of silver, for 'they took counsel, and bought with them the potter's field, to bury strangers in. Wherefore that field was called the field of blood unto this day' (Matthew 27:7, 8).

The hail dwindled suddenly, but stayed white underfoot, crunching like mothballs in the new sun. The field was tender with anemones and the stir of a dying olive tree. Here the Crusaders built a church, now gone, and the Knights Hospitallers raised a charnel-house for pilgrims on the scarp above, with bossed stones towering sixteen courses, their sky-eaten vaults still over them.

It seemed the nature of the valley to corrupt what was pure, so that even the supple flowers were ugly on its sepulchral earth, and the blood-coloured anemones tainted in their splendour. The fulfilment of prophecies of destruction can only be a matter of time – the ancient seers have nature on their side – but by an unpleasant chance prophecy has been translated literally in Gehenna. Graves have been re-used and desecrated 'till there be no place to bury' (Jeremiah 19:11), the dale scattered over many years with outcast bones. Travellers told of jackals and vultures even in this century, and crows still hover with furtive cries, and alight on their talons softly and horribly to watch.

Gehenna is deserted even now. As I climbed, Siloam was lost behind olive trees drowned in silt, and the village of Abu Tor appeared, named from a holy man who is said to have followed Saladin riding on a bull. Even the valley stream is thick and fetid, running in No-Man's-Land, and the orchards round it have grown old untouched. Birds rose from the steely waters where they have lived unharmed. Already barbed wire rusted among the pale camomile, and a notice read 'Stop. Frontier ahead. Danger.' At the entrance to Gehenna.

Ophel has been elusive even to archaeologists. Of all its centuries strewn about in stone, only a few can be deciphered. After Hezekiah the pageant fades again, though some foundations of houses remain from the seventh century BC, overhung by walls of half-shaped stones. Steps lead to a vanished terrace, and the remnants of a row of piers are fallen among clover where some hall had been, rather grand for its day.

Many figurines were discovered: primeval animals with graceless bodies and blotted eyes, cult images perhaps. There were clay women too, fertility symbols, with heads severely ringleted and arms cupped to their breasts: natural, pagan things – so tangible are the memories of Jerusalem's unfaithfulness.

Of the arts, music and poetry alone – the passions of the desert – absorbed the people, but these, like all else, were placed at the service of religion. No object of beauty has survived from their time and no tradition of craftsmanship, surrounded though they were by the skilled peoples of the world. Their energies were poured into their faith, and it is pleasing to be reminded by excavation that they used weights of pretty pink limestone, and kept their grain in bronze buckets, where shrews came to live and left their delicate skeletons behind.

The belief is ageless that disaster follows sin, and the Babylonian sack was seen as the vengeance of an offended God. The heathen statuettes are still eloquent, and the seventh century is dark with human frailty. Even the Temple was defiled by sun-worship and the ritual wailing of Phoenician cults. The ten northern tribes of Israel had disappeared more than a century before under the feet of Assyria, and in 597 BC, new from his northern conquests, Nebuchadnezzar seized Jerusalem and took away the leaders of her people. Ten years later, when Zedekiah, his vassal-king, rebelled, he came back and besieged the city for eighteen months, wrecked it and led away almost everybody in the land. The terraced dwellings avalanched upon each other, the ramparts were pulled down and the houses burnt, so that the stones are still heaped on the meagre walls where weeds of tired silver grow.

The Jews have left behind for ever the monument of that exile, poignant and savage as its time:

> By the rivers of Babylon, there we sat down, yea, we wept, when we remembered Zion . . .
> If I forget thee, O Jerusalem, let my right hand forget her cunning.
> If I do not remember thee, let my tongue cleave to the roof of my mouth; if I prefer not Jerusalem above my chief joy . . .
> O daughter of Babylon, who art to be destroyed; happy shall he be, that rewardeth thee as thou hast served us.
> Happy shall he be, that taketh and dasheth thy little ones against the stones.
> (Psalm 137)

Jerusalem, ruined far away, had grown into the Jewish spirit as symbol of its God and nation. History and religion were inseparable, each the expression of the other. The people did not attribute their defeat to the greater strength of Babylonian gods. They knew only their own. Because they had sinned, He had abandoned them.

The morality in their belief held them apart from others and its discipline preserved them. They turned in on themselves, cherishing their traditions, and almost alone among displaced peoples they were not absorbed. Fear may have played some part in this, and custom too, but above all, I feel, the secret was their own. How they acquired it is a mystery, and like history's other prodigy – the Greek mind – no explanation has yet quite compassed its miracle. Only their God, in all the world, had thrust through superstition to the heart, granting His people a new perception of sin, and offering as balm His holy laws. The star-gods of Babylon were senseless and puerile beside Him, and nothing in them could minister to the guilty soul of this ethically sophisticated people, cast out from its inheritance.

The quest of the Jews was for holiness, and because death brought extinction, their reward would be the mercy of God on earth. It is true that their Torah, their Law, is burdened with rules seeming petty or meaningless now, and fetishes which are known to desert Arabs still. But these are not its soul, which is a straining after righteousness, to 'be holy unto your God' (Numbers 15:40), and because its laws penetrated to the detail of ordinary living, they placed man, in everything he did, beneath the gaze of heaven.

How long the Jews could have kept their spirit one may only guess for, in 539 BC, Babylon was swallowed by the Persian Empire, and Cyrus, out of policy or benevolence, allowed them to return.

> When the Lord turned again the captivity of Zion, we were like them that dream . . .
> They that sow in tears shall reap in joy.
> He that goeth forth and weepeth, bearing precious seed, shall doubtless come again with rejoicing, bringing his sheaves with him. (Psalm 126)

Some of the Jews did not go back, for most of them had never known the city of which their fathers spoke, and Babylon was a fertile and comfortable land. Yet Jerusalem was slowly built again, more humbly, and the Temple with her, though the Holy of Holies was empty now and the Ark long vanished. Nearly a century later desolation still touches the words of Nehemiah, who inspected the ruined walls at night, guiding his donkey by terraces fallen so thick that 'there was no place for the beast that was under me to pass' (Nehemiah 2:14); but in fifty-two days he built them up again and withdrew the eastern bulwarks to the ridge of Ophel, laying the past to sleep under the quiet hill. A stretch of his heavy ramparts remains, but is poorly worked, for the defences were raised in urgency, and 'every one had his sword girded by his side, and so builded' (Nehemiah 4:18).

Israel's mission remained sure, chastened and deepened by her captivity. The pagan threat faded, the Law became supreme and, as if to sanctify her new purity, history and ruin slid away from the tired city.

Isaiah and Jeremiah had seen through chaos to light, when Judah would point the world to God in a Messianic age. Theirs was the classic concept of the New Jerusalem, a city made beautiful in the spirit, the fruit of man's growth to righteousness through the course of history. And if today this seems strange, it is not only because science has revealed complexities in human nature which render it, perhaps, incapable of such perfection, but because man has forsaken that easy intercourse with God which was familiar to the Jews.

They found Him by law and ritual, not questioning the mysteries of His Being, and the earthly paradise too was portrayed by Isaiah in the literal beauty which is special to Semitic peoples:

> And it shall come to pass, that before they call, I will answer; and while they are yet speaking, I will hear.
>
> The wolf and the lamb shall feed together, and the lion shall eat straw like the bullock: and dust shall be the serpent's meat. They shall not hurt nor destroy in all my holy mountain. (Isaiah 65:24, 25)

Yet here is only a terrestrial Eden, a practical dream, which can offer at most a life which is long and peaceful. After it the soul becomes *repha*, a shadow, so far from its Maker that Isaiah laments, 'Thou hast no praise in the world beneath, death cannot honour thee.' Thus man may glimpse his heaven, when for a few years he lives purely. Then his touch is severed, even with God, and the earth closes over him.

3
The Things which are Caesar's

The uppermost idea with Hellenism is to see things as they really are, the uppermost idea with Hebraism is conduct and obedience.

(MATTHEW ARNOLD)

La Grande sat in the hospice courtyard sewing, with rows of safety-pins fastened across her front.

'If,' she pronounced, 'we ever have a winter like the last one, I shall definitely drown. For two years somebody has been tampering with our weather.' She stared around suspiciously. 'Look. A rose has come out! After last winter that is a miracle. Did you hear about the snow we had? It was three feet high! It reached to my eyes!' She stood on the tips of her black slippers as if squinting over a monstrous tundra, and began boxing the air and burrowing through imaginary snow-drifts, then swept away the last flakes with a phantom broom. Like an earth goddess she embraced everything that lived, and her pots of plants were scrutinized like patients.

'One lemon tree grows and the other doesn't. What do you make of that? The sun is favouritizing.' She moved the pots about, small orange and loquat bushes, lilies and palms and white geraniums, and bound up the branches of the lemon trees with linen strips against the wind.

'And did you see? The canaries have had little ones. Four of them! Singing as they came!' Canary-cages dangled from every wall, and their mellow, constricted voices were the leitmotif of evening. In one cage was a downy pile of beaks and eyes, which opened soundlessly and looked afraid.

At night they were all moved indoors to sleep, and life in the courtyard dwindled to small, disgruntled sounds – the padding of erotic cats and the tinkle of the Madonna-like sister in the bowels of the kitchen. And much later there was no true noise at all, only depths and shallows of the night's silence: cicadas whispered from unseen shrubs, and lights were turned off one by one in curtained windows, leaving a sleepy confluence of stars, and the veil of the moon on the Dome of the Rock.

'In four weeks the *khamseen* will come,' said La Grande, '– the hot winds. Everyone gets bad-tempered then, if they were not already. But the big canary will hatch five eggs. She always lays five, punctually, three times a year. Are there canaries in England? In Poland there are scarcely any.'

'Poland is communist,' said Gentle Sister, as if Marxism and canaries could not co-exist. She was distributing food among them, occasionally putting a little into her own mouth. 'It is a land without belief,' she added sadly, her talk wandering between canaries and Poland. 'Here are three lady-canaries. And three gentleman-canaries over there in separate cages. Communism keeps everybody under. The world is really Christian. The gentlemen have to be kept apart or they fight.'

To Gentle Sister all was basically good. If people did not seem so, it meant only that they were smothered by an exterior evil, some historical accident. Through her wan, unguarded eyes she saw the world whole and fine, like a vision of Blake:

> For whether they looked upward they saw the Divine Vision,
> Or whether they looked downward still they saw the Divine Vision,
> Surrounding them on all sides beyond sin and death and hell.

She dropped some shredded carrot into a waiting beak.

'I was sixteen years in a convent in Hungary,' she said. 'It is happier in Jerusalem.' She knew the ugliness of mere system, and she loved the city, however cruel and troubled, because it was touched by holiness. These qualities go back thirty centuries as if cities, like people, never truly change. Feeling fiercely, profoundly, has left Jerusalem unbending, like a tree grown old, intolerance a foster-child of faith.

Once only, a milder light played across this harshness, after Alexander took the Persian Empire. For when he died the Ptolemies ruled Jerusalem clemently from Egypt, and the city felt the light embrace of Greece, the breadth and harmony of a new mind. Many of her people were beguiled by this rich and graceful culture, and as they learnt the Greek language they discovered also the concepts which it held, until the stern fabric of faith was sometimes loosened.

The Greeks, in turn, curious after novel states and systems, became intrigued by the Jews, and seeing them always engrossed in study of the divine, imagined them at first to be a race of philosophers.

To this time belong the tombs of the King's Dale, carved from the Kidron cliffs beneath the south-east walls of the city. The Book of Samuel says that Absalom, who rebelled against his father David, raised a pillar in the dale to perpetuate his name, and for centuries the northern monument has been called the Tomb of Absalom, though built long after him. The classical and oriental meet strangely here. Some bluntness in the sculptor's mind has cheated the façade of grace, although it stands in a Hellenistic mask, Ionic half-columns lifting to a Doric frieze; but above them the stone flies upward in a cylinder, whimsically elegant, like the snout of a stone tapir, and shrinks to a wisp of palms. One senses the closeness of Egypt, the decay of the Greek world, and recalls the loveliness of the spired pyramid which surmounted the Mausoleum of Halicarnassus, upheld on such slight pillars that it seemed to float in air.

The Arabs call the monument 'the Pharaoh's Tiara', and it seems that it was not a tomb at all but a *nephes* or 'soul', and was built to commemorate some family whose bones were laid in the hill behind, through a graceful, pedimented entrance. But over many years the Jews cast rocks at it, believing it to be the tomb of Absalom, and fathers brought their boys to show them what became of a son's ingratitude. So a hole was battered in the summit, and I climbed by cracks in the rock walls to its high entrance, and crept through an empty chamber in the cylinder where the light was drained to flax in arched recesses.

Another 'soul' was hewn out beside it, less fanciful than Absalom's, and heavily crowned with a pyramid. Some call it the Tomb of Zachariah, who was stoned to death in the Temple of the Lord, but the necropolis is empty, floored with dust, and garlanded in webs from wall to wall. A stairway goes steep and wide through the cliff's darkness, and meets a columned porch on whose lintel, rough and angular as children's scribbling, an inscription tells that these were the graves and cenotaph of the priestly house of Hezir.

Here is a giant strength unknown to other tombs, which shaped themselves to the slopes where they happened to lie. Whoever carved them so obstinately from the hill could not make them beautiful, only fumble with the arts of other lands, the Greek freedom still unborn.

So Hellenism lay on Judea, even after the Ptolemaic lenience was over and the Seleucid kings ruled Jerusalem in the second century before Christ. Never was there a more strange, portentous meeting of two worlds. The Greek, who trusted man with freedom, who saw the gods as blind or capricious, had discovered a people over whom ruled a moral Deity – an inner tyrant whom they insanely cherished. Even after polytheism was left behind, the Greek thought of God as immovable Being, abstract and indifferent. The obedience and discipline of the Jews fascinated and appalled him. How did this uncouth race come by such sureness in its knowledge of the Divine? The Jews' past had so endowed their present that the fount of their wisdom was holy revelation, not human reason. They studied the Law to live from day to day, and imagination, the bright genius of the Greek world, was forbidden them.

> Seek not what is too wonderful for thee,
> And search not out that which is hid from thee.
> Meditate upon that which thou must grasp,
> And be not occupied with that which is hid.
>
> (BEN SIRA)

The Greek had long ago doubted his own heritage. He listened to the world and interpreted it as it seemed to be. God was as fit a subject for rational discussion as any idle quality; no standard of excellence was in Him – 'Strive not to be like Zeus', wrote Pindar, and His heart at best was protean and cold.

In 167 BC Antiochus Epiphanes, fearing that Hellenism was drowning already in an Eastern sea, forced the new culture on Jerusalem, set up pagan worship in the Temple, and dominated it with a castle on the heights of the western valley.

Almost immediately the stricter Jews rebelled. The Maccabean family, priests and warriors, led them in a quarter of a century of war, and in 141 BC they stormed the Syrian fortress in Jerusalem. But now that the enemy had gone, the Jewish priest-kings, the Hasmoneans, proved militant and secular, and many of their people began to look for the establishment of the kingdom which was promised, the New Jerusalem. Then were formed the aloof and rooted Sadduces, deeply nationalistic, and the Pharisees, fervid for the Law; and the Essenes left the cities for the wilderness, awaiting the Messiah in lonely ardour by the Dead Sea.

Jerusalem spread westward and the Maccabeans built walls along the crest of Ophel, where a tower still stands, handsome for its time, and formidable. Beside it is a foundation-glacis of grey stone, and the old rooms which the Babylonians broke, the sadness of overthrow still on them.

All the centuries before Christ left themselves in fragments, bones under dust, and only stray lesions of the earth betray their presence. But the Romans built hugely, shearing away the grace of Hellenism in quest of the monumental or the simply practical. They came suddenly, devouring the Seleucid Empire, and Pompey took advantage of quarrels in Jerusalem to impose his will, propping up the last of the Hasmoneans as a client-ruler in 63 BC. Lenient and just, he plundered nothing, but out of curiosity he entered the Holy of Holies of the Temple, astonished at its emptiness, and the Jews never forgave him.

The act was symbolic. Down the years which followed, Rome dealt ignorantly with these closed, unyielding people; her mere presence violated their holiness and she flowed over them as water flows over stone, staining its softer parts but never touching its essence.

In the long reign of Herod the Great, her vassal-king in Judea, the forlornness of the task became clear. He was generous to the Jews throughout the Empire, raising them in wealth and dignity, but they never accepted him, for he was a foreigner, an Idumean Arab whose master was Rome. The city was branded with his gifts. The Temple platform is his creation, and after two thousand years it still covers the eastern hill, smoothing the rock's contours over the valley.

Jerusalem is a city of stone. The ramparts crush her inward, blinded with sun, and the streets run breathless and hostile, creases on the rock's hand. The beautiful forests vanished long ago from these hills, so that roofs are domed or vaulted now, and shutters are of iron. Scarcely a tree grows. Walls climb high on every side. The sun marks out the paths in shadowed or dazzling steps, and grinds the summer earth to power on the hills.

Near St Stephen's Gate, where the cistern Israil has filled with earth, the northern side of Herod's Temple ran. An angle-tower slumbers on monster ashlars half in earth, and where I went south along the Ottoman walls, the smooth rims and jagged bosses of the Temple blocks burgeoned through the grass. 'Master,' cried the apostles, 'see what manner of stones and what buildings are here!' (Mark 13:1)

Ten thousand men were picked for their construction, and a thousand priests trained in the craft, so that they alone might erect the inner sanctuary. They began in 19 BC and eighteen years later all but the final touches were accomplished. The inner court and holy house exactly reproduced the size of the Temple of Solomon, and their doors, like his, were panelled in gold and silver, even to the jambs and lintels. But the whole enceinte, a mile in circuit, was larger far than Solomon's, and twice the size of the temple which it replaced, built on the return from Babylon. Josephus called it 'the most prodigious work that was ever heard of by man', and in many places where I walked the stones lay twelve feet in length or more, until the tanned Turkish blocks seemed light as pebbles over them.

In AD 70, only six years after the Temple's perfection, the Romans threw down all but these imperishable depths of stone. They are only like the heads of swimmers whose bodies rest beneath the sea. They have been found to plunge unimaginably deep – forty, ninety, more than a hundred feet beneath the Moslem and Crusader dead, reaching to some core in the earth's warmth, where the hill itself has been notched to receive them. But those above the ground are substantial and beautiful. Each is different like a face or hand; one sees the precision or roughness in its finish, the little inequalities of surface, like skin, the patinated colour and the wandering of the veins. Two millennia have damaged each according to the softness or strength of the rock from which it was taken, so that some have been mutilated by the wind, and others, though delicately cut, are as smooth as ever they were.

I walked high above the Kidron through the bosky Moslem cemetery where graves stood like tall, pale beds, abandoned, and anemones knocked their red chalices on the marble. These are the sepulchres of virtuous men and women, some of them famous, allowed within the shade of holy walls, where the resting of the poor is marked with a few rocks.

There were graves by the walls even in Herod's time, and a bridge spanned the valley over them, to keep those passing from the taint of bodies. High above, his Temple had spread like a kremlin, more superb than beautiful, but glistening in new limestone, in the long reach of its pilastered courts and upsurge of wide towers. Around its platform, pierced by many gates, thousands might sit in the Court of the Gentiles, whose hosts of columns shed a tiger shadow; and beyond the doors of Nicanor and the Court of Women, where teachers sat and only the pure might enter, the Holy of Holies shimmered on the sky with beaten gold. Jewesses, who could go no further, clustered to see the great altar, and here Mary must have stood with her child to be purified, and 'to offer a sacrifice according to that which is the law of the Lord, a pair of turtledoves, or two young pigeons' (Luke 2:24).

I lay on the wasting earth, looking at the Mount of Olives where it went down into the valley. Goats were tinkling round about, and near my elbow a chameleon crawled, his spongy hands extended from blade to blade of grass in a sly, fastidious gesture of escape.

The Golden Gate was nearby, which Moslems call the Gate of Eternity, but it has been blocked for four centuries. Through it, in happier years for Christendom, the emperor Heraclius brought back the Holy Cross from Persia, and Christ may have ridden on the first Palm Sunday. Seen from without, it is only a handsome tower with the ghost of a great gateway, but within the walls is a six-domed vestibule, built by the empress Eudocia, perhaps, in the fifth century.

I found it closed by iron gates. A cat fled up the pilasters on invisible paw-holds, and the noise of birds echoed in the locked hall with the secret of their entry. Through holes in the gates I looked into a pure Byzantine world, or so it seemed, a pale, grey chamber, one of the loveliest in Jerusalem, carved with the feathered touch which the Moslems were soon to make their own. Its cupolas, strong and light and low, once covered the passing of Crusader processions – the Feast of the Cross and the Day of Palms – and here and there were the stones of Herod, by which Christ had come, and ashen columns lifted to the ceilings.

Other pillars had been thrust by the Turks through the outer ramparts to bind them, and Moslems claim that one, projecting far out, will be the throne of Mahomet at the Last Day. Here the Herodian blocks are lost, so high-banked is the earth, and the walls are Ottoman from earth to sky; but at the south-east angle the great stones rise again, immaculately dressed, each set back a little from the course above, and extend more than a hundred and fifty feet, nearly half beneath the ground. The Evangelists called this the Pinnacle of the Temple, and wrote that Satan held Christ there in a vision and tempted him to cast himself down unharmed; and a few years later St James, it is said, was thrown from it to his martyrdom.

The southern walls move heavily, framing the blinded gates of Herod's time. The Pharisee historian Josephus, who knew the Temple in its brief prime, calls this the Royal Portico, triple-aisled and double-storeyed, with carved roofs and a hundred and sixty-two Corinthian columns. He remembers the Temple roofs with their golden spikes to fend off birds, the portal of the sanctuary wide open 'for it symbolized the all-seeing eye of heaven' (Josephus, *Wars of the Jews* V.v.4), and its veil of mystic colours.

Behind it Herod's fortress rose, cruelly dominant. He never comprehended Judaism, but with a sense more Roman than Semitic, envisaged a Jewry secure and honoured in the fold of a worldly empire. The stricter Jews knew this, and hated him. Even his generosity was an embarrassment to them, and their holy books mention him only once, as the man who imported a new breed of pigeon.

The Roman rulers of his day held him in respect, indebtedness or affection, which shows, perhaps, that he belonged to their world more aptly than to Judea. Despite his subtlety, his political flair and his knowledge of men, his loyalties were genuine and his shrewdness and resource were threatened by a quick passion. Almost to the last Mark Antony was his friend. It was he who had the senate declare Herod king of Judea in 40 BC, despite the enmity of Cleopatra, and Herod, when called to account after Antony's defeat at Actium, did not disclaim him.

Yet Herod never understood the land he ruled, only the empire he served. None of his earlier buildings in Jerusalem – palace, hippodrome, amphitheatre – prepared the Jews for his undertaking the new Temple. So little did they trust him that some suspected he would raise a pagan sanctuary or a shrine to Augustus Caesar; and perhaps Josephus guessed his motive when he said, in passing, that the Temple 'would be sufficient for an everlasting memorial of him'.

Now the confusions are dead two thousand years, and Herod's vision is reality: Judaism set in a civil state. Small boys, half Bedouin, plant leeks below the Temple walls, and watch them sprout with idle, forsaken faces. Stray tourists notice only an upsurge of large stones, the thistles' angry thrust on long-closed doors.

On Herod's esplanade – a vast and paved near-emptiness – the Dome of the Rock alights from the sky, so sudden and harmonious its beauty. The Arabs call the plateau *Haram es-Sherif*, the Noble Sanctuary, and every part is adorned with their legend. But the spaces around it, too great for the Dome, have been turned to orchards and gardens, and covered in fountains now silent. Search beneath the ground, and even the entranceways are there: the gates which Christ and his apostles knew. They reached the Temple across the Tyropoeon – the Outer Valley – on viaducts from the Upper Town, or climbed to it by rock-cut steps. Three of the entrances are known, and the American scholar Robinson in 1838 noticed the stub of a huge arch which had led into the Royal Stoa, its stones eroded so strangely that the Jews declared it to have shuddered and compacted when it heard the ancient sages in debate.

A larger viaduct, named 'Wilson's Arch' from the British archaeologist who first studied it, lay among debris north of the Wailing Wall, but I could not find it, and took to wandering through the Moslem quarter, asking for 'the great bridge of Herod'. People showed me foundations near their homes, bestowing diluvian ages on them, and one man said that Herod was an old friend of his, but that he had recently left for Amman. Hearing that the arch lay among ruins by the Wailing Wall, I applied to the representative of the Grand Rabbi for permission to explore, expecting to see a snowy patriarch happy to grant my request in absent-minded benevolence; but instead I met a young man, who scrutinized my untidy Gentile person while I spoke to him in bad German. This, translated into Yiddish, sounded like a declaration of war, and permission was refused.

But I reached the arch soon after – a forty-two-foot span – great trunks of stone now scarcely heaving clear of the soil. Looking down a shaft dug more than a hundred years before by the archaeologist Charles Warren, I saw that the Temple walls preserved their beauty underground almost to the bed of the Tyropoeon. The arch itself enclosed a cistern of clear, cold water, where Mahomet brought his mare to drink after riding her through the air from Mecca. All about were sewers and passageways of many ages, leading beyond where I could safely go, and the viaduct, crowded with Arab and Crusader arches, passes through ten or eleven leaps.

The other gates were guarded by the Moslems, and for four days I returned to the Temple area with requests to see them, and was shuffled between lesser dignitaries like an unwanted cat. Responsibility spiralled upwards from imam to sheikh to cadi, until I stood in the office of the Mufti of Jerusalem.

The Moslem religious leader is different from most others. He is both pastor and politician, and because Islamic law is still operative, he may be judge and legist as well. The dignity of office clothed the Mufti like a spell. In his face the eyes were questing and richly arcane, as in a man whose avenues of thought are many. Beautifully turbaned, immaculately robed, he motioned me to sit, listened in silence to my requests and granted them with a princely smile.

He sent an imam to guide me – a huge, speechless person to whom all doors were opened. In the south-west we searched for 'Barclay's Gate', descending to the underground Mosque of Burak, disused as long as could be remembered. Against its side only an iron ring glimmered, to which Mahomet tied his magic mare, but on the darkness of the western wall I touched giant stones. The imam struck matches for me, mumbling that there was nothing, and from the Rembrandt light a monster lintel grew, and other blocks moving inward in a smooth arc cut off, where worshippers had climbed the valley steps and reached the Temple through a sunken way.

We went down to the vaults, 'the Stables of Solomon', which held up Herod's platform in the south, descending through a crypt in the weight of the Temple walls; Christ and Mary, it is said, hid in its darkness on their flight into Egypt, and an upturned Byzantine niche is shown as the Child's cradle. These substructures, restored in Arab times, seemed too fine to have been other than the aisles of a church or palace. I walked among their eighty-eight piers as through a rotting forest, while the imam lumbered softly behind. The Crusaders used them for stables, leading in their horses and camels through a modest, Gothic entrance, now immured, and I saw where the knights carved mangers out of the ground, and smoothly bored their tethering-holes in stone.

Dank and close, it must have been insufferable in summer with its flies and stench and weft of trodden dust. The imam coughed in disgust and shuffled his feet. I listened to the drip of water, knitting the stones, and watched the light's deceit as it cast the shadow of each pier upon the next, thinning and multiplying them into the dark.

Then the doors were locked behind us and we mounted again to the dazzling courts which had once been Herod's. New doors were unbolted and we saw beneath us, sloping southward, an arcaded ramp of darkness through the earth. The imam stood guard in the entrance, leaving his monstrous shadow on the steps, and I descended alone.

This Double Gate, and another to the east, were the old corridors called Huldah, 'the Mole', which tunnelled from Ophel under the Royal Stoa to the Court of Gentiles. A Jewish legend told that they would outlive the ruin of the Temple and would last until it was built again. Since the century of Christ the way has been blocked, and nowhere else may one walk so closely to that time. The sunlight shrinks to a ripple in the window, and the pillars stand as Josephus described them nineteen hundred years ago, each so thick 'that three men might, with their arms extended, fathom it round', becalmed by their own strength. Gauntly they loom in the empty gates, sentinels of its quiet, raising capitals and cupolas whose carving, though whitewashed by the Arabs, still shines through with a dry, fastidious beauty. The way is dim and sad, like a place dreamt, where Christ trod upward to the praying courts.

In a city where trees and birds were frowned upon, Herod's palace, soft with doves and gardens, was an outrage or a balm, according to temperament. High on the rim of his swelling metropolis, he hedged it with three towers 'for largeness, beauty, and strength, beyond all that were in the habitable earth' (Josephus, *Wars of the*

Jews V.v.3) and named the two strongest from Hippicus, a friend, and his brother Phasael, both dead. The third, more slender and more various in the rooms which adorned it, he called after his favourite wife, Mariamne, a beautiful Jewess of the royal Hasmonean house; but all were ravaged by civil war in AD 70, long after his death, even while the Romans were besieging the city.

The Crusaders rebuilt them as an inner keep, extending the ramparts to the west, until Ibn Daud of Kerak pulled the fortress down in 1239 and the Mamelukes, and the Turks after them, raised a new castle on its buried stones.

Now fir and fig trees grew in the shadowed moat as if they still fed on water. The barbican – a playful, slightly ridiculous gesture of defence – stood where a vanished drawbridge reached across; above them the glacis straightened to walls, and many towers thrust heavy and secretive to the sky.

Inside, the ramparts looked on empty courts, sparrows splashed among wildflowers, and hollowed rooms made tracings in the grass. Here Herod laid his gardens cool under porticoes, with groves and walks where water, channelled out of Bethlehem, flopped from brazen statues into pools. At the base of the Citadel's keep, called the Tower of David, his blocks were massive and beautiful, fifteen tiers above the grass; for the Phasael tower has remained, and its forbidding vastness, even without the testimony of Josephus, betrays that Herod was afraid.

He built hugely for his defence, cresting the steepness of valleys now smothered, and only when his towers were firm below, jointed like single spurs of rock, did he hang turrets luxuriously above them and spread his gardens in their shade. Yet some secret violence in his nature refused him peace. His suspicions fell first on Mariamne, victim of a plot which only his jealousy could not perceive, 'for his love to her was not of a calm nature, nor such as we usually meet with among husbands' (Josephus, *Antiquities of the Jews* XV.vii.7). She had rejected him – he had murdered members of her family – but she was never unfaithful, and went serenely to her death. The moment she was gone he fell into demented grief, weeping and speaking tenderly to the air, and ordering his servants to call to her as if she were still nearby; and long afterwards he commanded banquets and celebrations to drown her memory, but could not, 'being deeply in love with her in his soul' (Josephus, *Antiquities of the Jews* XV.vii.2).

His life grew steeped in evil, in the blood of Pharisees burnt alive, of three hundred army officers stoned to death, of his own sons strangled on false suspicions. The palace courts were haunted in those last years, where the stones of Phasael rest their sad strength. Excavations have uncovered layers from early Hasmonean times, revealing that he was not the first to build here. Finer blocks were laid in the last years of the second century BC, and may have buttressed the tower which Herod raised to Hippicus, for they are hideously fissured through holding up a weight too great for them.

The Tower of Mariamne is lost, the Crusader gates and stables almost buried, but the Ottoman walls are pleasant to walk on, with their windy embrasures slotted for the beams of a missing gallery; and some Roman fragments have been left between the moat and the eastern gate, where a little mosque stands open to the sky.

A black rabbit browses among Herodian columns. An arch spans no way. The dusk deepens on the flower-filled earth. In his declining years Herod passed in and out of madness, and well may he have ordered the massacre of innocents at the rumour of a child-king in Bethlehem, for he was so ill that his blood was poisoned and his body filled by maggots, and he could no longer limp into his gardens nor climb the bulwarks named from those he loved.

From the southern parapets the finger of a minaret points to God, and as I mounted it I saw the western walls swim out on the waves of the hills. The square of the Armenian Gardens grew small and green below, and the Bastille turrets of the Church of the Dormition dwindled to toys. Only a fern tree, softer than an eyelash on the earth's floor, remembered the wind. Yet even from here the citadel was formidable, and I wondered how the Tower of Phasael had seemed when it stood at twice this height, built to the scarp of heaven. Far to the east the Moab hills keep the Dead Sea at their feet, where the dying king was rowed across to the sweet healing springs of Callirhoe, which could not heal him.

4

The Fall of Jerusalem

And from the daughter of Zion all her beauty
is departed: her princes are become like harts that find no pasture, and
they are gone without strength before the pursuer.
(Lamentations 1:6)

The year glided to its brief spring – 'We travel to God' as Gentle Sister murmured – and the sun muted and faded everything in the hospice. Each evening I escaped the mixed fury and languor of the streets and slipped through the courtyard door as into a warm bath, hearing the low chant of the nuns from their chapel, like contented bees.

All that they had missed in life appeared to mean little to them, for their lives were only the porch to a great house. Because they were sure what lay beyond, they felt no need to love the world for itself, but waited quietly in their vision. Being happy as well as serene, they remained individual, but from time to time their routine was disturbed. Thirty Franciscan monks arrived for breakfast on the feast of Our Lady of Poland: dark, stout men, shaped like skittles, who rolled comfortably in and out of the refectory, with bottles of wine. The Monsignor of the Polish community travelled between his separate concerns, and I would see him at sunset, walking in prayer along the veranda. And there was Hanna, a very old man, almost blind, who was given food when he visited, and would turn his clouded eyes from the door before leaving, and thank the world which he could not see in meticulous, old-world French: *'Merci. Merci, infiniment.'*

An American Jesuit passed through from India with two snakes in his luggage, which he made drink from his basin. He was worried because one would not slough its skin.

'If they don't slough, they die. It's like getting rid of *sin.*'

Carefully we plucked the brittle film from the beautiful, subaqueous body, while it eyed us indifferently and opened a hard pink mouth as if to speak. I kept wondering what would happen if one of the nuns appeared and saw us fondling this emblem of Satan. La Grande would probably garrot it with a rosary. But at last it sloped glistening into the basin to drink, god-like and repulsive.

'That means it's well,' said the priest, and left its clouded and redundant coat in pieces on the floor, where the sisters must have found it.

Ten orphan girls danced in the courtyard's dappled sunlight, with a noise of fairy gaiety. They were kept by two young Polish sisters, who sang in the little chapel, their voices dark and strong against the harmonium, whose notes flowed into the courtyard. Here the children stood wide-eyed, and La Grande nodded and smiled in speechless enthusiasm.

The nuns understood the orphans well. Their own Slavic warmth helped them to sympathize with the wayward and despotic habits of Arab children, but they managed severity from time to time, and taught hard work and independence. Their foresight and discipline were subtly passed on, together with that interest in things for their own sake which must be a hallmark of civilization.

In the Middle East I grew to love the Hellenistic passionately, not because it was more beautiful than elsewhere – it was often coarse and hybrid – but because it shone through a tangle of servility and mindlessness, in art and in life. It is old-fashioned to attribute civilized traits to a Greek legacy, and the Arab's inquisitiveness and a certain scurrilous levity are all his own. Only where the academic intrudes, or an unsensual, abstract love, did I suspect an alien heritage, and came upon it with surprise and gratitude.

The pious Jew saw the Greek world wholly evil, and it often reached him in decadent forms. The Greek and Roman, in turn, came to resent the Jew's separateness, which is, perhaps, the root of 'anti-Semitism'. '*Odium generis humani*' (Tacitus, *Annals*) accused the affronted Roman – they had a hatred of the human race – for the man who stands apart inflicts unwittingly a slight upon the rest of humankind and may kindle an urge to discover or to destroy the secret so closely kept.

The Jews fought Hellenism with the rigour of the Law, and by the time of Christ had built around each precept a nest of rules and observances so far-reaching, so articulate and so minute, that no part of life was free of them. Each action was governed for the service of God, but often this web degenerated through the poverty of man's nature into habit and ritual, smothering the spirit which it might have enhanced.

Should one eat an egg which had been laid upon the Sabbath, wondered the pious doctors? The hen had broken the rule of rest and had gone about its normal business with a vulgar disregard for the Law. Was a little girl found on a dungheap in Jerusalem to be considered impure? She was, said the pious; and emancipated slaves were unclean for a generation. Might one squash a louse on the Sabbath? The sterner minds said No; the more indulgent declared that the insect's legs might be removed. Such legalism left many tiny avenues of escape and through these, seeping away unnoticed, went love and humility.

Yet the Pharisees were conscientious guardians and teachers, and their view was more open and happy than that of the Sadducees, who saw no future for men beyond the grave, and no mission for Judaism outside its own people. The Pharisees, however canting and loveless some of them may have been, believed that the individual soul would be answerable to God hereafter, and they contrived to guard their people against all foreign evils, and to build the Law so strong and fearful that two thousand years were not to break its hold.

In Jerusalem their time was running low. Roman procurators ruled Judea ten years after Herod's death and were less tolerant of religious foibles. Herod Agrippa, his grandson, held a brief kingdom from AD 41–44 and built out the northern palisades on the lines which the Turkish walls still follow. To their north-west he erected the Psephina fort, whose foundations bulge in the cellars of the Collège des Frères; and under the Damascus Gate an arch of his northern entrance has been found, flanked by the worn feet of columns, and a sober, magnificently jointed tower. From the lowest tip of Ophel he strung ramparts to meet the southern walls, where his long, paved streets remain, and so in four years, though his work was stopped by the suspicions of Claudius, Herod Agrippa more than doubled the size of the fortified city.

The monuments left over from these times are those which were embedded in the very fabric of nature – tombs cut in the rock. It is sad that the most enduring monuments are also the most depressing, and a morbid aura lingers over my memories of days spent rummaging among places of fetid secrecy.

My most flagrant violation was of the 'Tombs of the Herods', which look across the old No-Man's-Land from the valley of er-Rababy, whose rock is fine and soft for carving. Their name is glamorous enough to attract stray tourists, but they may have belonged to any Jew who was Romanized and rich enough to build them, and the entrance is barred.

A round stone had been rolled back from the mouth of the tomb and awoke a vague disquiet in me, some reverberation from the Christian subconscious. I squirmed down the slit above it, unsure if I could climb out again, and walked through chambers whose sides were of dressed limestone, blemished in my torch-light, and covered with a whining gauze of flies. The ceilings were crimped to harmonize with chiselled walls, and above them a decorative and complex monument had stood, and left scraps of cornices behind. It is not known who was buried in the vault, but it looked across, when new, to Herod's towered palace, shining and remote in the western walls; and Josephus writes that members of his family were entombed nearby.

In these days men died in less sadness. Traditions reflected in the later books of the Old Testament had hinted at the immortal soul, and the Pharisees developed them into a doctrine of hope, unconsciously preparing the way for Christ. So the dark crypts, with their cenotaphs and sunken courts, were not always seen as graves, but as places of waiting, where the soul, as Job had prophesied, would be clothed again in flesh to meet its God.

A more lovely tomb was built by Helen, Queen of Adiabene, who crossed from Mesopotamia in the first century AD and became a Jewess. It lies behind walls in a fork of roads, where I entered a quietness more imagined than real, seeing the elements of silence everywhere – flowers and grass – and heard birds singing. I went down a rock-cut stairway thirty feet broad, more like triumphal steps than a descent to the grave, and saw the grooves of aqueducts sloping to full cisterns in the greying cliffs. Lizards slumbered affluently on the cushions of their bellies, and poppies mounted the stone, trembling with night rain.

An arch led to the courtyard where a whole palace appeared to be sunk in rock, lowered away from the tread of living. So huge a cavity could not have been cut to serve as the vestibule to a tomb but must have been a quarry long before, shaped to symmetry by the architects of the queen. A high porch darkened its western face, the columns gone, where the rock was startled into life – grapes, wreathed crowns and lyre-shaped acanthus. Columnated spires, elegant in an aura of spurious classic, had crowned the tomb where now the eye met only sky and trees, and had left their sculptured fragments in curious heaps.

A stairway delved below the porch, and the grandeur dwindled to a tiny dark entrance, where in a groove a softly weathered stone was rolled away. Pausanias, in discursive mood, mentioned this grave where 'once a year on a fixed hour and day, this stone moves by itself, exposing the entrance to the cave, and shortly rolls back of its own accord' – a chance fable, perhaps, collected from some local dragoman. But behind the stone, disclosed by ruin, is an unexplained chamber where a crouching man with a heavy wedge might easily have worked the grisly miracle.

The queen lay safely buried down a secret vault until the last century, when an archaeologist, believing that he had detected the tombs of the Judean kings, discovered her sarcophagus and took it away to the Louvre. Her history, like so much else of this time, is learnt from Josephus, who says that she became wife to her brother, who fell in love with her, and was converted to Judaism after his death. Queen of a land in league with Parthia, her charity saved Jerusalem from famine, and Izates, her son, kept her faith even on the throne. His religion turned his nobles against him but he was successful in war, restored the King of Parthia to his realm, and was rewarded with the rights of the King of Kings: to wear a high tiara and sleep in a golden bed.

He died shortly before his mother, and the new king 'sent her bones, as well as those of Izates, his brother to Jerusalem, and gave orders that they should be buried' (Josephus, *Antiquities of the Jews* XX.iv.3). Eighteen hundred years later her sarcophagus was opened, and she was seen preserved in the dry Judean air, her arms crossed on her breast; but she crumbled instantly away, leaving only the golden threads which had lined her shroud.

In the wolf-light of the necropolis the air grows gaseous and close, and the graves thicken under stairs descending to new halls, where *arcosolia* are cut, and *loculi* to receive ossuaries and the oven-like recesses called *kokhim* – all stagnant and dismal among weeping walls, so that I was glad to find the sun again and feel the wind.

Westward I crossed the valley where the old border ran, past the narrow Dale of Walnuts and the 'Tomb of Simon the Just'. Already through the waste the tracks were beginning to move again, like insect paths returning to the bed of a lost river, asserting the ancient rule that man must meet and make exchange if he is to live. Here the Arab women, hands raised to the burdens on their heads, walked stately through the grass, keeping in the flow of their stride and upright bodies the grace of pastoral ways.

I climbed to the Tombs of the Judges, where small-headed cats slunk down funerary paths. I felt guilty again, like an ancient tomb-robber. Graves seem to have been carved up to the time Jerusalem fell in AD 70, but the feeling of pious quietude remains, pervading the banded entranceways, the ledged benches for funerary feasts, the steep descent of stairs, and rock-cut pools where doves live. The tombs wear the classical dress lightly, as a gesture, round pediments of eastern tumult and clumsy columns; and the bodies were laid in a friendly Semitic proximity, the doors gone now from the stone lips of their shafts.

The 'Tomb of the Sanhedrin' especially, betrays its Roman entrance by a tympanum of Syrian ornateness, and inside, the *kokhim* are close in tiers, and stairways burrow left and right so that I gave up crawling through them and sat outside on rocks musky with blossom and unopened flowers. Here at the northern limit of Jerusalem the valleys fell empty, cloud-laden and blunted by mist, where drops of sunlight lit inconsequential rocks.

Water, cutting deep in stone, has left a broken spoor where the Romans channelled it or renovated older works. Centuries before them an aqueduct snaked casually along the western hills from Bethlehem, where the Pools of Solomon are jungle-green in spring, and send their brimming river down its course to slop at last into the basins of the Temple area. The origin of this aqueduct is unknown, though the Book of Ecclesiastes says that Solomon made gardens and orchards at Jerusalem, and 'pools of water, to water therewith the wood that bringeth forth trees.'

The Upper Aqueduct, financed by Pontius Pilate from the revenues of the Temple, was more practical, thrusting straight and deep and resting in covered pits before it met the older channel at Jerusalem. In places it can still be seen, jutting in severed veins from the slopes of Mount Sion, but it was abandoned long ago, more vulnerable in its Roman disregard for landscape than the older way, which yielded, eastern fashion, to the strength of things around it.

A branch of Pilate's channel may have fed the Citadel, slipping from the pool of Mamillah which lies in a Moslem graveyard outside the western walls. This pool is pure, sea-colour, cut in rock, but I can find no mention of it before the seventh century AD, when the Persians filled it with the bodies of martyred Christians. Legend tells that a kindly lion carried the corpses to a nearby cave, where a church was built and lies in ruin. Whoever lay in this cemetery, ran Moslem lore, would reach the lowest heaven, but half of it has been grassed over for a public park and the rest is forsaken, haunt of many birds. A scattering of pretty grey domes covers the bodies of various notables including, it is said, the jester Johha, whose puns were rather a trial; but the graves scarcely show above the tall and paling grass where Crusaders were buried before them.

The waters streamed out to the ancient Serpent's Pool, which the Crusaders widened to the Birket es Sultan and Suleiman adorned with a fountain, and flowed to the city underground, falling into the Pool of Amygdalon, old even in Christ's time. This also has remained, fetid and brown most of the year, and enclosed in a square of houses high as cliffs, whose mottled stones are dotted with cats and washing. Walking along Christian Street, I saw its strange reservoir from the back of several shops, and a tiny woman with Delft blue eyes lured me into her house to see it. Hers was an enchanting home, early Ottoman I think, with wavy floors of roseate stones and alveolar windows. The stench from Amygdalon – now called the Pool of Hezekiah – scarcely reached her windows, and she brought sweet coffee and biscuits, rather stale, and talked politics, grabbing hold of the imaginary throats of many well-known statesmen, and delivering *coups de grâce* with a teaspoon.

It is hard to know how old these pools may be, since waterways, like roads, die hard. The poets praised the city for her many springs but this was in hindsight, and of all her waters only the Gihon fountain is alive. The Pool of Bethesda merely collects the winter rains, and the Bath of the Virgin Mary is forgotten, walled in tumbling stones. Here the lion-coloured battlements go north in serried towers, no house or person near, only the green earth flowing to their buried feet. I saw the pool in early summer, its sides ruffled by tadpoles, and small frogs swam in peace, the thrust of their new-found legs cutting bright blades of sunlight after them. A swift, in vanity, touched his reflection on the water's surface, and broke it with a light splash where he drank, graceful even in this.

I slept there in the sun. A man came and threw stones at the frogs, which is often the Arab way, who sees the world as his theatre. I wondered if the two paths could ever meet: the subjective and passionate with the reasoning and reflective, Jerusalem with Athens. Of all the cities in her empire, Jerusalem gave most trouble to Rome. Others accepted the *Pax Romana* with a good grace. In Syria and Phoenicia the Semitic images were thrown out of the temples, but their spirits returned, clothing the classical gods with cosmic attributes, and the *mésalliance* was a happy one. 'The island of Tyre has nursed me,' sings an assenting voice, 'but my motherland is the Attica of the Syrians at Gadara. An offspring of Eucrates and a companion of the Muses . . . Is there anything untoward in my being Syrian?' (Palatine Anthology vii.417).

Why, the Romans wondered, should the Jews not also conform? What was wrong with them?

It was a time of visions and portents. New Messiahs appeared and were crushed. When the procurator Gessius Florus rifled the Temple in Jerusalem and killed several thousand citizens in AD 66, the Jews rebelled. The Roman garrison was slaughtered as it marched under armistice out of the city, and the army of the Imperial Legate was chased from the walls. All over Palestine and Syria the Jews and pagans fought.

Nero sent Vespasian from Britain to quell the revolt, and Titus, Vespasian's son, came north from Alexandria to meet him. One by one the Judean cities fell before their armies, seventy thousand of the finest soldiers in the world. In their monastery above the Dead Sea the Essenes gathered their sacred scrolls and hid them in caves before they fled away; and the Christians, an obscure sect of Jews, escaped northward and over the Jordan, for the Master had warned that 'When ye shall see Jerusalem compassed with armies, then know that the desolation thereof is nigh. Then let them which are in Judea flee to the mountains . . . and Jerusalem shall be trodden down of the Gentiles' (Luke 21:20, 21, 24).

Vespasian, meanwhile, had left for Rome to assume the purple, for Nero was dead and three makeshift emperors followed him. But in AD 70, at the time of Passover when a million pilgrims filled Jerusalem, Titus arrived outside the walls and spread his legions to their north and west. As the priests entered the Temple on that holy night, wrote Tacitus, the earth quaked under them, the great doors of Nicanor swung open of their own accord, and the ghostly tumult of an invisible people was heard to pass through them, crying to one another to depart.

Even as the Roman battering-rams moved against them, Zealots, robbers, fanatics and priests massacred one another within the walls, prolonging a civil war which had been waged for three years. Titus attacked from the north as other conquerors had done, and by early May had stormed the first two ramparts, and settled down to starve the city out, enclosing it with blocks of plundered stone which are still scattered in a crescent through the suburbs.

His offers of surrender were rejected. Famine and robbery spread over the city, so that many people crept outside to gather herbs, and were caught by the Romans, some five hundred every day, and crucified in grotesque postures until there was no room left to plant the crosses round the walls. Whole families died of hunger, and the dead lay unburied in the streets or were thrown over the parapets into the valleys, where Titus saw them heaped and 'called God to witness that this was not his doing' (Josephus, *Wars of the Jews* V.xii.4).

Yet the Jewish soldiers still repulsed the Romans at the rock-like walls and sallied from the gates. Starving, they chewed belts and sandals and the leather from their shields, and a woman roasted and ate her own child. A kind of madness seemed to have settled over the chiefs, who refused every plea to give in, 'no gentle affection touching their souls' (Josephus, *Wars of the Jews* V.xii.4). Within a few months, wrote Josephus, seven hundred thousand people had perished in the city, their corpses stacked in the locked houses, and many deserters were caught by Arab mercenaries, who believed that they had swallowed gold, and slit open their bellies. The Romans themselves were becoming sickened and angry.

At last the Temple itself was reached, and for almost a month the armies fought for it. Titus gave orders that the sanctuary should be spared, but in the final sortie a soldier, lifted on the shoulders of a comrade, flung a firebrand into the Holy Place.

For the rest, it is told by Josephus, who was present. 'And since Caesar was unable to check the passionate fury of his soldiers, and the fire was spreading, he went with his generals into the Temple's holy place and saw all that was in it, which he found more wonderful than the tales of foreigners, and equal to all that we ourselves had believed and boasted; but since the flames had not yet reached its interior, but were raging in the chambers round about, Titus rightly supposed that the shrine itself might be saved, and ran to persuade his soldiers to put out the fire . . . but their fury was greater than the esteem in which they held their Caesar . . . and one of them hindered him as he ran to restrain them, and cast fire on the gate's hinges in the dark, so that the flames leapt out from the holy house, and Caesar and the generals retired, and no one any longer forbade its burning; and thus was the holy house destroyed, without Caesar's assent' (Josephus, *Wars of the Jews* VI.iv.7).

Jerusalem fell in the beginning of September, after one of the most sad and savage sieges in history. Titus spared only a fragment of the western wall, and the three great towers of Herod's palace, their charred stumps lonely and high where the city was a ploughed field. Some sacred vessels and a golden candlestick, rescued from the Holy Place, were carried in Titus' triumph through Rome, and are preserved in sculpture on the arch which the senate voted him, still standing in the ruins of the Forum.

The Temple at Jerusalem was never built again and, except for the short reign of Bar Kochba, the Jews did not return for nineteen hundred years as masters to the city.

★

The Damascus Gate is the threshold to the Old Town; her other gates are sturdy and useful, but are like the wings to a theatre, whose centre-piece is this immense and fanciful portal, built by Suleiman the Magnificent in the vigour of the Ottoman age. Through it the flow is turbulent and full: peasant women in their long, embroidered dresses, foreheads which ripple with golden coins; the mingled patience and disquiet of Arabia.

The east is warm in its exclamatory façade and in the street, the Khan es Zeit, which channels the harlequin torrent through its way. But the Moslems call the gate *Bab el-Amoud*, the Gate of the Pillar, and the street keeps a Roman straightness, a needle pushed through something dense and old. A column, buried to its neck, slopes from a shop or wall, pointing the tendril of an ancient way, choked by the resurgent east. Sixty years after the fall of Jerusalem Hadrian, ever the passionate Hellenist, began to build her up as a pure pagan city. The Jews revolted under the fanatic Bar Kochba, and were only crushed after three and a half years. The emperor called his city Aelia Capitolina – from his surname, Aelius, and the Capitol – a reminder to the people of where their allegiance lay, and the Arabs call her *Ilya* even today.

Hadrian stretched his colonnaded streets from triple gates, in the majesty and logic of Rome. Across the western ridge, where Semitic alleys wandered, he thrust his *Cardo Maximus*, the backbone of a classical city, and bent another road down the Tyropoeon valley. These, whittled to threads, are today the Khan es Zeit and the El-Wad, and are clear on a Byzantine mosaic map at Madeba in Jordan, meeting at a memorial column long since disappeared, which gave its name to the Gate of the Pillar.

Hadrian saw his city as a monument to reason in the soil of superstition. It would lie with grace and order on the home of a people whose mark of faith was to enslave the mind and circumcise the body. He forbade the Jews ever to enter it, but peopled it with Gentiles from districts which had not known this madness for the One God, and gave it almost the measurements which the walls keep today; built a theatre, a circus, a forum and a mint; temples to Jupiter and Juno. He set up statues on Herod's ruined plateau, which he excluded from his city, so that the Jews came to weep against its walls; and perhaps to obliterate the memory of a Christian holy place there was raised 'a dark shrine of the unchaste demon Aphrodite' (Eusebius, *Life of Constantine* iii. 25), where two hundred years later Constantine claimed to have found the sepulchre of Christ.

Aelia Capitolina has left itself piecemeal behind: the milestone of the Tenth Legion which supports a street lamp; a tetrapylon turned into a café; the emperor's laurelled head in stone, of tired nobility; the broken words 'Colonia Aelia Capitolina D.D.' still carved on the arch which he rebuilt beneath the Damascus Gate; and through the Russian Hospice Alexandre the dimpled Roman flagstones spread, used to the open sky, and the western arch of Hadrian's forum stands in the incense-haunted air.

Before medieval times another arch was seen on the site of the Antonia fortress, where tradition claimed that Christ had been condemned to die. Pilgrims, believing it to date back to his time, called it the arch of Ecce Homo, where Pilate, finding no fault in Christ, led him out before the people and cried, 'Behold the man!'

In 1857 the ruins were bought for the Sisters of Sion, who raised a church around the gateway; but archaeologists later realized that the arch was typical of the three-bayed gates which spread over the Roman Empire in the second century. It was the eastern entrance to Aelia Capitolina.

The Sisters of Sion, with the practical intelligence of their order, have accepted this, and as it is the genius of religion to turn its earliest beliefs to symbols, they have kept their arch enshrined. The church stands spellbound over it. Nowhere else is the new so kindled by the old. Scars have become beauty, and the patina of centuries lights up the stone in its past, reaching beyond form and touching imagination.

It is a side-entrance only, a gate for pedestrians, and the centre arch passes through the wall beside it and over the street beyond. The sisters assemble early for Mass. The windowed dome has scarcely received the morning. The white-veiled heads are bent and quiet, until a switch is turned and the gate is plunged in light. Their chanting rises unbodied. A gold mosaic stars the apse. The dazzling head-dresses stoop together, and the sunlight grows like a ghost until the arch is almost standing in the Roman day. One sees the niche where a pagan god had stood, and a Byzantine *graffito* above it: a faint web of lines where the boorish name can no longer be read.

The passing of the classical mind from Judea is nowhere more poignant; for on Hadrian's city, sterilized for two centuries, the east was to break back – Christianity, Byzantium, Islam. Meanwhile, Hellenism could not share the Jewish vision. It dreamt of no New Jerusalem unless of Plato's perfect city, an ordering of streets and intellects for the attainment of Absolute Good. God stood wrapped in an eternal self-communion. Time was an inane cycle, goodness the child only of knowledge.

Yet life was full enough to divert the mind from the shadows which stretched beyond it, and the times were busy and prosperous, even for a city deprived of the *civitas romana*. As the temples of Aelia rose on their sacred hills, the Jews took away their vision with them. They had only to trust and obey. 'The end of the matter, all having been heard: fear God, and keep his commandments; for this is the whole man' (Ecclesiastes 12:13). But they wondered, as the centuries lengthened, what sin had brought such punishment upon them, and why Jerusalem had fallen. The sages answered variously. Some thought that the Sabbath must have been desecrated, some that the fault lay in the morning and evening prayers; but others said that their city was destroyed because the Law was founded only on observance, and was not interpreted in the hearts of men.

5

Quest for Righteousness

I have loved you with an everlasting love;
therefore I have continued my faithfulness to you. Again I will build you, and you shall be built, O virgin Israel!
(Jeremiah 31:3, 4)

Already in the hospice the lemon trees were shedding their blossom, and the vine which had straggled along its trellis flowered into a tent of parrot-green leaves. At evening the convent's cat attracted an armada of toms, which would cruise over stairs and walls with tails raised derisively, until La Grande erupted from the shadows with a broom.

As the heat increased, her detonated questions grew slower, and Gentle Sister's disembodied replies nearly faded away. The sister who was always laughing took to wearing white, and was invested with a new serenity. The baby canaries grew old enough to sell to the Jews, and the big one laid its five eggs punctually as La Grande had commanded.

Laughing Sister's activities were mysterious to me for a while. In the hospice courtyard was a small room with a bed. Three or four times during my first week I saw her disappear into the room in the company of different men, her face crossed with a dulcet smile. After about ten minutes she would emerge again, still smiling, the man sometimes pulling on his jacket as he went. All this happened in so matter-of-fact a way that at first I thought nothing of it. In the Father's house are many mansions, and that of Mary Magdalene must be one of the most gracious. But the problem was solved by a line of old women which entered the hospice one morning calling for the clinic, and the sister took them blithely to her room, not knowing what absolving thoughts were sliding over me. She was, in fact, a trained nurse, as I might have guessed from her efficient, sprightly ways, and the Pontifical Mission sent medical supplies, which she used judiciously among the local people.

She and the Madonna-sister took me one evening to their hospice in the New City. I had become curious about this, since they were always talking of it with longing and enthusiasm; it was 'big', 'modern', 'clean' and 'wonderful'; but now they seemed afraid that when I saw it I would want to leave them and stay there.

'Old buildings are more beautiful,' said the Madonna suddenly.

They walked on either side of me through the dark streets, like escorting penguins, their starched headbands luminous under the black veils. They had come the same way often when the barriers stood between Jordan and Israel. Houses which had been emptied twenty years reared their carcases about us, and a *khamseen* cloud showed violent on the sky, carmine with the last sun. We walked through an imaginary Mandelbaum Gate – nothing now but a few concrete obstructions piled like clods on one side of the road.

'There were mines here,' said Madonna. 'You know. Boom! They were blown up as soon as the war was over. We were so relieved that we danced there! All over the rocks!' She flapped her arms, and under that strange sky I imagined the whole Polish Sorority leaping like fauns along half-detonated mine-fields.

'We're here,' said Laughing Sister. 'Sssh.'

'Why sssh?'

They said that they did not wish to see the sisters. It was too late to be sociable. We slipped in by a fragrant garden. They flicked on lights showing long passageways full of doors, hygienic and practical, with none of the wrinkled intimacy of the older hospice.

'Look at those beautiful corridors!'

The penguins flitted up and down the stairs, their voices tinkling covertly as they led me to the chapel and the roof.

'See. They even have a vegetable garden,' said Madonna.

During the June war she had listened from the rooftops in the Old City, hearing the guns at night near the new hospice, and had watched the flares falling. She wondered if her sisters were still alive; but the shells had only hit the garden walls. For a while we sat on the terrace looking down at lights and at the illumined clock-face on the tower of St Saviour's, suspended in the night. When we crept down again we found the door locked. They confabulated in panicky whispers. Then out came a cheerful nun with a round red face like the Queen of Hearts. She gave them a huge box full of shoes, which were to be distributed among poor women in the Old City, and with this we plunged back into the streets. The shoes were high-heeled, except for an odd, right-footed slipper, but later I heard La Grande address it determinedly: 'We will find you a one-legged woman!'

It was the Sabbath evening, and Jews were walking back from their synagogues through the dark. The sisters tried to avoid them, slipping round by quieter streets, because the Orthodox sometimes spat on their dresses and frightened them.

The shadowed figures went softly by, silhouettes on half-lit walls. Already I felt angry. Others moved towards us, curled side-locks dangling from the wide hats. But they passed.

For a time I was insensitive to the differences among the Orthodox, though I watched them praying at the Wailing Wall, the western rampart of the Temple. It is less a wall complete in itself than an audience of stones, some – from the hard *mezzy* strata – keeping their Herodian rims so pure that they run evenly together; others, plucked out of the soft beds of *malaky*, waste away until a block is split inwards through its whole thickness. At noon the sun holds them in a blinding curtain; the *khamseen* awakens and whirls the prayer-shawls round the faithful and rolls the dust about their feet. But evening grows gentle on the stones, shadowing every wound as a painter brings subtlety to primal colours, and arc-lamps pick out shrubs which fall theatrically from crevices.

The men crowd to the wall, their heads scarcely reaching to the second course of stones – Hasidim and Mitnagdim, sunless under their wide hats; ashen spirits which seem to see only their own souls. They touch the wall's roughness with their hands, their faces, and the heads begin to sigh, swinging up and down in a rhythm beaten by their minds, their ringlets knocking on their cheeks and necks. The scrolls of the Law are unfolded on rollers from velvet sheaths, and a confused, unhappy rumour, half chant, half sob, grows from the base of the tremendous stones. Sometimes it swells to a roar of misery, a man shouting a song, a chorus despairing after him:

For the palace that lies desolate.
We sit in solitude and mourn.

For the walls that are overthrown.
We sit in solitude and mourn.
For our majesty that is departed,
For our great men who lie dead,
For the precious stones that are burned,
For the priests who have stumbled,
For our kings who have despised Him . . .
We sit in solitude and mourn.

Yet more often a wordless nostalgia, a *Weltschmerz*, pervades them, something older and more permanent than the sorrow for an exile or a temple lost. The eyes are cast down as the holy books demand; only the heart uplifted. The lips kiss the rock. Two thousand years have wept there, such grief as would touch anything but this immovable stone.

With naked hands they tore the granite,
and the centuries with them
echoed their sorrow, murmuring in it,
'O lost Jerusalem.'
(EDMOND FLEG, *The Wall of Weeping*)

Where they wept at the time of Hadrian I do not know, but Constantine, it seems, permitted them to return to the Temple, for in AD 333 a pilgrim wrote that 'the Jews come each year to a perforated stone which they anoint, then lament with groans and tear their robes and depart' (Travels of the Pilgrim of Bordeaux).

Soon after, the emperor Julian attempted to rebuild the Temple, but the ancients said that balls of fire erupted from the foundations, and whirlwinds and earthquakes chased the workmen away, while opaque crosses, added Christian writers, were imprinted by magic on the robes of the Jews.

At the end of the fifth century the ruined precincts were again proscribed, and after the Jews had called down the Persians in AD 614 and caused an awesome destruction, the Christians heaped dung on the sacred stone – perhaps the hillcrest covered now by the Dome of the Rock – for it was all there was left to defile.

The Moslems gave the Jews protection, and in the eleventh century fifty families were living in the holy city. The Crusaders massacred them, but in 1163 Benjamin of Tudela found some two hundred living as dyers under the Phasael Tower, and already a 'Juiverie' had grown up north-east of the city. Twenty years later the community had dwindled away, but Saladin allowed them to return, and thereafter a small group was always to be found.

Yet the spirit of the Jews was nursed in other lands. Since the time of Nebuchadnezzar they had fanned across the Mediterranean in a diaspora which the sack of Titus turned into migration. Philosophers in Egypt, merchants in Greece, physicians in Italy, few were the vocations to which they did not turn. They carried their hard, familiar ways with them, cherishing their heritage as a fountain in the emptiness. Thus the thread which linked them to the past was never broken, so whole, so disciplined, so internal was their world. Blind to the ease of peoples round about, they accepted their punishment and promise as the stamp which God had set upon them. This, and persecution, were the secret of their survival. Every thought and action was bound in the faith which the Pharisees had left them, so that divinity pervaded the ordinary paths of living, minute by minute and century after century. 'One walks in holiness across the fields, and the soft songs of all herbs, which they voice to God, enter into the song of our soul. One drinks in holiness to each other with one's companions, and it is as if they read together in the Torah' (Martin Buber, *Hasidism and Modern Man*).

A whole tradition grew up on the Old Testament – the Talmud and the Midrash, commentaries and illuminations, covering all aspects of man's life. Their dialectic is sympathetic only to the Jew, and even the *Haggadah*, the Talmud's strain of parable and legend, points to such finespun moral as seems petty and archaic to the glance of an outsider. Yet beneath the network of precept, strong but invisible like the current of a river, are the concepts of man's free will and sanctity, the emphasis on good action and a withdrawal from philosophy alone; and the significance of a text, it is believed, may never be entirely revealed, but holds its last meanings beyond understanding.

Jerusalem, as time and distance blurred her, was sharpened in myth. No evil could enter her walls, no roof fall in, no fire erupt; and those who mourned for her would see her resurrected. Death was but a name there, for her earth was the hall to heaven and was sprinkled beneath the Children of the Diaspora in their foreign graves. The sacred instruments of the Temple had never been destroyed, but lay where kings and prophets had hidden them in the blue depths of fountains, with the golden harps fashioned by David and the jewel which Moses carved from the throne of God.

But the pilgrim to Jerusalem, tired with the Mediterranean waves, the tracks of Syria, found that his was a dream city. The Moslem centuries covered it. On some empty hill he first prayed in its sight, and rent his garment; but behind the walls rose a sheaf of minarets and a cloud of Christian domes. For him there was only the bitterness of a falling temple, crowned with a foreign god.

Yet buildings could neither buy sanctity nor dispel it. The footsteps of his fathers were warm on the stone. Jerusalem kept his past and his future, and he came to her in the spirit of return, in recognition of his father's earth.

The Rabbis, in their matter-of-fact way, said that a man must recite a verse from Isaiah and rend his garment when he first sees Jerusalem, and rend it again when he glimpses the Temple. 'The formality should be carried out standing; it should be done with the hand; the rents should be extended until the heart is laid bare; and they must never be sewed up again.' A man should bring into existence no perfect thing, but leave a fault in it in memory of Jerusalem; so that his stuccoed house will show a barren patch, and his banquets lack some delicacy.

Jerusalem – *Yerushalayem* – a name 'as sounding as the cry of trumpets yet as sweet as a shepherd's pipe' – three times a devout Jew still faces her and pleads to God: 'And to Jerusalem, Thy city, return in mercy, and dwell therein as Thou hast promised. Rebuild it in our own day as an everlasting dwelling.' And as the Passover prayer reaches its climax, he voices the immemorial dream: 'Next year in Jerusalem.'

A legend tells that each part of the Temple was built by a separate class and that the paupers raised the Wailing Wall. While the city was being sacked, and the other courts and buildings were falling in flames, angels touched it with their wings, proclaiming 'This, the work of the poor, shall never be destroyed.' Holiness still keeps a hidden presence there. On dewy nights the stones are seen to weep for the destruction, and a white dove mourns.

I do not know how long it has been so sacred. Benjamin of Tudela wrote of it eight hundred years ago. An Ottoman sultan, runs a tale, granted it to the Jews as a seat of worship, but for years the Moslems had made a pious habit of tipping refuse there, so he scattered coins over it and poor people, searching for them, cleared the rubbish away. The wall is as deep beneath the ground as it is high above, and rises to the rimless tiers of Hadrian's city, to Turkish and more recent layers; but seven courses from Herod's Temple are still visible, and these are holy to the Jews, though built by the king they hated. Between the joints of the ashlars they thrust their written prayers, sure that God will not refuse them. General Dayan, after entering the captured city in 1967, left the petition 'Let peace reign in Israel'; and flatly declared that 'We have come back to our holiest of holy places, never to be parted from it again'.

So the Wandering Jew returned. He stands there, if he is Orthodox, pouring his ageless longing on the stones. To those who do not understand, there is something disquieting in such drunkenness of grief; but he keeps it secret to himself, turning close against the wall as in the privacy of anguished love.

For him the return of Israel is scarcely begun. Other Jews have set their hands to the building of a new state, but he must await the Promised One, who alone can bring Israel into her heritage. Nothing is valid, nothing is fulfilled, until this Saviour comes. Only warfare has brought the pious to Jerusalem, and the Defence Forces of Israel, he feels, do not constitute the Messiah.

The liberal Jew looks on this sorrow as on an old love, with embarrassment and faint surprise at the feelings of his past, and suspects ritual lamentation as an oriental cult.

Around the wall the land was levelled in 1967, the dwellings bulldozed away; and shops and a plastics factory were demolished nearby with military urgency, so that Arab businessmen were later seen scrounging in the debris for their accounts. On the scarp above, the old Jewish quarter begins, savaged twice by war in twenty years. Rabbis came from France and England to live there after the Crusaders had gone, and gradually the 'Juiverie' in the north-west was abandoned. Jews from Spain and Central Europe followed, and their property expanded until by the end of the nineteenth century the sector held fifteen thousand people. Again it is being rebuilt. Everywhere I heard the tapping of the demolisher's pick, the drip and thud of plaster and stones. Dust, white and fine as a mist, stifled the ruins.

I met a Jewish girl there, who had known the quarter as a child before 1948. She walked in confidence – a girl of barbarian beauty – speaking of streets where I saw only rubble, remembering houses, synagogues and friends. Here and there a Hebrew notice hung on a locked door, telling whose home it had been, and whose it would be again.

'The people will come back,' said the girl. 'It will be built again as it was. It is part of our soul.'

Arab children, refugees before, stared at us with alarmed eyes. In the Street of the Jews we went into Ramban, the oldest synagogue, built by Moses ben Nahman who came to the city in 1167. 'We found a ruined house with handsome marble pillars, which we converted into a synagogue,' he wrote, 'for the city is at the disposal of anybody – no one in particular being able to lay claim to it.'

This bare, foreshortened chamber, curved round its columns sunken in the floor, became the core from which the sector grew. A synagogue was built beside it sixty years after, and inherited the homely name *El Maraghah*, 'Where donkeys roll', and the Ashkenazim, Central European Jews, worshipped here for generations with the oriental Sephardim. In the eighteenth century many were exiled and their synagogue decayed, so that it was called Ha-Hurva, 'the Ruin'; but it was reopened by Sir Moses Montefiore and Alphonse de Rothschild, and gave scholars to the Jewish world.

Through its corridor we walked into a hard, bright cubicle of ruins, and climbed beyond the courtyard of the Tree of Life to the heaped sanctuary by the ascent of a broken arch. We went down other streets and saw the synagogue of Bethel – a black door and a musty hall – where the Cabbalists had worshipped, and the old cry was long remembered: 'O how great and fearful is this holy place, where the lions of learning dwelt in all their glory!' And on our right sprawled the sanctuaries of Johanan ben Zakai where the 'horn and olive-oil of the Temple' were once kept, with the stone 'seat of Elijah', whose ghost had joined the Sephardim in prayer.

As we walked, the city died. From the overcrowded refugees' houses we came on empty dwellings, courtyards of grass and broken light. Some artery was severed nearly unnoticed, the nuance between home and ruin. Painted doors lent a milder air of habitation, stencilled with flowers and domes by pilgrims returned from Mecca; but suddenly we reached a part which had dissolved into debris as at the touch of a hand. The dust steamed under us. The whole sector rolled in a grotesque turmoil at whose centre a small boy was seated like a penitent seer, throwing earth upon his head.

Once the houses had been built sturdily by Dutch and Germans, and in 1948 two thousand Jews had shut themselves up in them to fight, deserting the other dwellings, which were thus preserved. When they surrendered they left behind eighty-six dead who lay buried in the rubble of the Misgav Ladach hospital, and their precious scrolls, since vanished.

Quaint in survival, a lantern jutted from a wall; electric wires wandered; a stone bench had once been set in shade; and the girl walked moodily until I too began to imagine the white dust shaped again to the needs of the living. Yet soon nothing will remain but a memorial or two. Already a *Yeshiva* of boy students was studying in the wreckage. The unmanageable earth was being trundled away in barrows, and after twenty years the dry click of chisels has startled the limestone from its glittering sleep.

We sat in a phantom synagogue while the afternoon wore itself out, leaning against the walls where the dissenting Karaim sect, powerful in the Middle Ages, had dwindled to three men. We gazed at the Pride of Israel synagogue opposite, founded by Sephardim in 1872 and said to be lovely then, though even in its waste too ornamental.

'The emperor Franz Joseph came here once,' said the girl, as if she could remember him. 'The "Pride" was not yet complete and when he asked why it had no roof the Jews answered that it had taken off its hat to the Emperor. He took the hint and paid for the roof. Nice old man. But I don't believe any of it.'

The sun relented, and children, out of school, hid and conspired together, so that as we walked away all the ruins were giggling.

The New City has no such air. It has scarcely a building older than a hundred years, and keeps everywhere a light uncrowdedness. Especially in the south it nudges along spurs and valleys, and I could not tell which was a suburb and which a hamlet. The Hebron road went by the old frontier, where every yard was sprinkled with concrete and shards of iron. To the north the clean, geometrical rush of the New City faded, and the old one blended to earth, releasing here and there a tower or cupola, the golden hemisphere of the Dome of the Rock.

When I crossed the southern quarters the vista disappeared and I walked in the vale of Rephaim, where giants had lived, and where David descended on the Philistines while the wind of the Lord went before him through the mulberry trees. Beyond spread the sleepy solidity of the Greek Colony and the ridge of Katamon, with the Valley of Roses still green; and above it a church covered the legendary tomb of St Simeon, who took the Christ-child in his arms in the Temple and uttered the lovely canticle: 'Lord, now lettest thou Thy servant depart in peace . . .'

The Protestant Templars, who once owned the German Colony, were shipped to Australia in the Second World War, leaving only the convent of the Sisters of Charity by which to remember them. The houses are of limestone and pleasant with trees, and the roads bear the names of those sympathetic to Jewry: 'Rehov Emil Zola', 'Rehov Lloyd George'.

A railway runs to the east, and beyond, sloped to a view of wasted hills, I saw the Convent of Poor Clares, a closed order founded by the disciple of St Francis. For the past nineteen years the building has stood almost in No-Man's-Land, and the nuns still weave vestments and walk in high-walled gardens. Two of them communicate with the world on behalf of the rest, and they showed me their church and the outer court, where I sat for a while on the scented pine-needles, sleepy with their incense and the feudal quiet. Somewhere I heard laughter thinned by many walls, but saw only doves flying with stalks in their beaks, iron-barred doors and the still pines.

To the north the Hebron road emerges from its outskirts to the heart-city, walled Jerusalem. However expected, however known, its coming is awesome, lifted on bald, undulant ridges, the square towers of Suleiman shadows in the sky. Beneath it Montefiore built the earliest Jewish suburb, Yemin Moshe, in 1860, with a Kentish windmill which is now a shrine-like museum. Behind is the towered

YMCA, the graceless bulk of the King David Hotel and the Pontifical Institute, while to its south St Andrew's church and hospice, built in memory of Scottish soldiers killed in the Great War, stands on its hill alone. A tomb with a man's skeleton is sunk near the doors, and visitors were often taken down to see him in a friendly social spirit, until some fastidious person sealed him up.

The church is pale and simple, and in the passageway nearby is a pair of seventeenth-century Florentine gates exquisite in wrought iron. The pews are carved with homespun Scottish names, the altar rests on green-veined marble from Iona, and in the chancel floor, polished discreetly golden, a plaque reads: 'In Remembrance of the Pious Wish of King Robert Bruce that his heart should be buried in Jerusalem. Given by Citizens of Dunfermline and Melrose.'

I stood looking at this, and at the bright, unhaunted church, remembering schoolboy history: that the king had asked for his heart to be laid in the sacred city where he had never trod in life. Sir James Douglas, carrying it to the Holy Wars as he had been commanded, fell fighting the Moors in Spain, and the heart was brought back and buried, it is said, in Melrose Abbey, while the king's body still lay at Dunfermline.

In the New City every kind of Christianity is keeping a foothold. There is the Ratisbonne Monastery, drunk with oleanders in May – the foundation of a Jewish convert; the blitzed Notre Dame de France where iron girders have dangled twenty years; and a painted Abyssinian church, whose priests sleep in the gardens in their black gowns with long black cats around them. A Russian cathedral is airy and baroque, its hospice walls silenced, whose pilgrims were the poorest and most fervent in Christendom; and a giant pillar rests beside it, perhaps hewn for Herod's Temple, but before the carving could be finished it cracked across and so preserved itself, and lies now in a bed of fading roses.

Dominating the Mamillah road, the Soeurs de Charité de St Vincent de Paul live in a labyrinth of corridors and halls, where they keep an asylum. The tiniest nun I had ever seen came to guide me, blessed with the energy of the very small. Down the aisles of the great church she bobbed and curtseyed to wax saints and Virgins, intent on showing me the statue of a canonized sister of the order, wearing the flared-out head-dress which was recently abandoned. It was this which excited her.

'Look at that! A white starched veil! When we first came here the Ottomans thought we were birds!'

I walked down penitential passageways, the little nun alighting around me like a snowflake.

'But those old veils were impractical. When we were in a bus, we looked to the right. Piff! We hit somebody. We looked quickly to the left. Piff! *Voila un oeil poché!*'

We came to a courtyard in a fierce wind and she was almost blown away into the oleanders, and then we were back again in the long gloom, from whose rooms the madwomen who are kept here looked out at us with happy, brutal faces.

'When we took children to the cinema everybody complained', she continued oblivious on the subject of head-dresses. 'You could get your money back if you sat behind a Sister of Charity! But then' – and her voice tapered to a reverential whisper – 'His Holiness the Pope gave us a dispensation. We were blessed. We were permitted to change.'

Under lines of shrunken washing – a last gesture from provincial France – she let me out into the street. I sensed, somehow, that she had preferred those old veils.

I stood at the hub of the New City, where the old roads of St Louis and Princess Mary have changed to more national names. Even here the uncrowded, half-built feeling remains, as if the whole modern town were a suburb to nowhere.

It is, in reality, an emanation of the walled Jerusalem, built to partake of its magic. Yet its aspect is wholly Israeli. It has no élite shopping centre, no fashionable boulevard, and a motley collection of cars goes through the streets. A democratic energy pervades it, as of a society too threatened to resolve into classes other than those gained by a man's worth. In this urgency buildings have gone up quickly, and limestone houses, which were compulsory on the Jordanian side, are mixed with stucco flat-blocks. But the Schocken Library is pleasing in dark lemon wood, still keeping its old books in the sunset light which its architect, Eric Mendelsohn, intended; and the Hebrew Union College, though poorer built, shows also this simple, pleasing blend of wood and stone.

Spread to the city's west, beyond the residential suburb of Rehavia, are the buildings of its university, its parliament and its great hospital, but they are the new signs of its inspiration whereas I was searching for the old.

Northward I passed the Great Rabbinate, enclosing a cluster of offspring organizations, presided over by the Chief Rabbis of the Ashkenazim and Sephardim, whose power is yielding slowly to that of the schools of religion. Beyond them were the limbs of Zionism: the Jewish Agency, the World Zionist Executive, the Jewish National Fund, the United Israel Appeal; and beyond these again, the unlovely Yeshurun Synagogue, largest in the city, where I stood one morning at the hour of first service.

Some thirty men were scattered among its rows of seats in mumbled self-communion. Their worship was so muted and informal that I could not discover where the prayers began or ended, but an American Jew came to my aid, running a finger along the English text. Apart from him, the men appeared to be mesmerized in the grandeur of tradition. They were almost all old, their prayer-shawls dripping tassels from their shoulders, small blocks bound to their foreheads, and their wizened left arms tied in the *tefillin* straps; for the *Shema*, the closest the Jews know of a creed, asks that 'ye shall lay up these my words in your heart and in your soul; and ye shall bind them for a sign upon your hand, and they shall be for frontlets between your eyes'.

One of the congregation guided their prayer, facing the Ark, where scrolls of the Law are kept, and where a tapestry portrayed the ancient Temple in a shining fall of silk. But they prayed as if they were alone, whispering to their hearts, some even walking about, rapt and zealous.

The service was steeped in praise, mounting swiftly to the lovely words which a Christian, in his doctrine of original sin, can never utter: 'O my God, the soul which Thou gavest me is pure . . .'

They spoke less to a Father than to a King, distant yet closely known in His commands, a Majesty untouchable but a law in the soul. And soon came the grateful sigh: 'Blessed art Thou, O Lord our God, king of the universe, who hast not made me a woman', while a sprinkling of women, segregated on the balcony, said charitably: 'Blessed art Thou, O Lord our God, king of the universe, who hast made me according to Thy will.'

A remoteness, a reticence, lay across their worship, for the Jew does not rest on God as his personal redeemer and rarely pleads a passionate absolution, but stands before Him in the dignity of an obedient heart. And surely no nation has offered such praise to God: 'Though our mouths were full of song as the sea, and our tongues of exultations as the multitude of its waves, and our lips of praise as the wide-extended firmament; though our eyes shone with light like the sun and the moon, and our hands were spread forth like the eagles of heaven, and our feet were swift as hinds, we should still be unable to thank thee and bless thy name . . .'

Time and again some spectre returned from history in their words, and at the end those who claimed descent from the priests of the Temple mounted the dais, drew their shawls over their heads like men miming ghosts, and pronounced a blessing.

Their worship is without music, but is itself a hymn, a harmony of poetry and thought. On the Sabbath there may be song without accompaniment, and the psalms of David take again their nationalistic fervour, a dawn vision of the world, and the gratitude which is the natural expression of the Jew to God.

'The search for enlightenment,' a rabbi told me, 'is our only real mission – the quest for righteousness, which means that it is important above all to learn. A peasant does things because his father and grandfather did them. His life is like a fulfilment of ritual. But the more he studies, the more a man will understand. Freedom will grow in him.'

He was a cautious rabbi, for six years a pupil of Leo Baeck who looked sideways at me from a photograph on his study wall; and when I mentioned his master the rabbi smiled and softened, and talked to me as a friend. His was an immemorial Jewish face which stared at me from not far above the top of his desk, so small was he; and in the darkening light of the room the discs of his glasses glowed in loneliness, like owl's eyes, and his high forehead creased itself to arabesques.

'It is the task of learning to make us conscious of the spirit,' he said, 'and all true learning must, as its last aim, bring us closer to God, nearer to holiness.'

But were not so many rules of conduct, I asked – voicing an old disquiet – in danger of smothering the truths beneath them?

'The danger is immanent,' he answered. 'It is the duty of study to dispel it.'

I could not answer. I am not sure if people can be disciplined into loving. 'What is a charitable heart?' wrote Isaak of Syria. 'It is the heart of him who burns with pity for all creation – for every human being, every bird, every animal, every demon. He looks at the creatures or remembers them, and his eyes are filled with tears.' Could such freedom be fashioned from the science of the Law? Once a man's freedom falls from him he ceases to be fully human. The peril of so much observance is to stifle both good and evil, until there remains not even the lesson of suffering, the sacrifice of a broken spirit.

The rabbi seemed to know what I was thinking. 'Men who lived as long ago as Jeremiah and Ezekiel understood that obedience was not itself righteousness,' he said. 'But we ask dedication to the Law first, and understanding to follow after. The Law will itself bring spiritual perception.'

He spoke a slow, untainted English, like a man who feels the responsibility of his gifts.

'We look upon God as one might look upon a teacher,' he said. 'This is the mystery of tension: between the distance of God above us and His closeness in our souls; between our fear and our love. Each man, you see, was created divine, yet has it in his power to neglect that divinity. For man is both great and small in God's presence, made "a little lower than the angels", and he too may be a creator of goodness.'

He pointed his pipe-stem at me.

'We have not this belief in original sin. We have not this conception that we must all be saved; except in a Messianic future. The Hebrew word which you translate as "repent" in reality means "return". If a man sins he seeks forgiveness of his neighbour and returns to what is good.'

So practical a path is deeply Jewish, and the concept of a simple turning to righteousness – which is also the Islamic way – removes all that may be passive and morbid in sorrow for sin. I wondered how deeply guilt is felt or salved by this disarming ease.

The rabbi gazed through the blue whorls rising from his pipe, like a friendly oracle. 'And because inherent sin has no meaning for us,' he continued, 'we find no need of missions. I recognize the right of everyone to observe God in his own way. Other religions are not my concern.'

'But if you believe yourselves to be in possession of truth,' I asked, 'how can you withhold your truth from other people?'

'We do not withhold. But others must come to us, not we to them. We should live so well as to be witnesses to Israel and to God. But our God is not the saviour of the individual soul.'

'I don't understand you.'

'I mean that the whole idea of saving is foreign to us. It is our duty to prepare for the Messianic age, when Israel will be fulfilled and her higher truth made evident.'

His words seemed to glide back through the centuries to the intense, close nationalism of Judea, and for the first time, like the plucking of a string inside me, I felt resentment.

'You wouldn't feel the Jewish way to be so excellent that it must be imparted to the Gentiles at once?' I asked.

But he answered ingenuously that it was very hard to be a Jew; and although I thought that this was a poor escape, I knew it to be true, and later remembered that the religious of Israel believe they will uplift to God not only their own nation but those who for two millennia have chosen to persecute them.

The light had almost vanished in the room, but the rabbi seemed not to notice, and remained a disembodied face in the gloom and smoke, his skull-cap pressed back comfortably above a pair of spatular, goblin ears. 'And as for missions here,' he said, 'we have suffered much over the centuries and have reached these shores to build up a state. We did not do all this in order to become Christians! But we feel, we know, that the future is good. All history is an unfolding . . .'

In his momentary smile there flickered the age-old Hebrew patience, the New Jerusalem awaiting her Messiah, the trust which bore up a scattered people in the weight of the blind world, so that nineteen centuries after the sack of Jerusalem a Jew could still scratch on a cellar wall in Cologne: 'I believe in the sun even when it is not shining. I believe in love even when not feeling it. I believe in God even when he is silent.'

★

To the older Jewish communities in Jerusalem were added those from Yemen, who first arrived in the sixteenth century and who are known for their delicate jewellery, their love of poetry and song, and for their honesty. Persians and Moroccans came, and despite the Ottoman law against Jewish immigration, the congregation in Jerusalem more than doubled in the middle of the nineteenth century. Of the two older groups, the Sephardim have been outstripped by the Ashkenazim, who continued to filter in from Poland, Germany, Russia and the Balkans, and though once despised were always the most enterprising of the Jews and have now risen to a dominant position. Persecution in this century quickened their coming, and Jews in Arab countries, disturbed by the growing anger in a world which had generally been tolerent, have appeared in swelling numbers.

The Israeli, it is said, has lost all the characteristics of the Jew in exile, but even if this were true there remains in the city the dark side of his mirror, an eidolon from the centuries he endured. Dressed still in the black clothes of the ghetto and the peasant fields of eastern Europe, the ultra-Orthodox live in poverty in a half-walled suburb of northern Jerusalem. Almost the first to leave the safety of the inner city, they established the quarter in 1875 and called it Mea Shearim, 'a hundredfold', named from the increase which was granted to Isaac by God on the land which he sowed (Genesis 26:12).

Their days are engaged in study and worship. They receive money from relatives and organizations in Israel and abroad, while their wives earn what they can. Pacifists awaiting the kingdom of the Messiah and disinterested in the modern state of Israel, they consider the Hebrew tongue too holy for every day, and speak Yiddish, a mixture of Hebrew and medieval German. A few mean shops and a market are the centre of Mea Shearim, with dark, crushed houses stretched on empty streets. Notices caution strangers to dress modestly and to remember 'the virtues of the Jewish woman through the ages', and the women wear their 'headscarves and thick stockings with a modest dignity', and keep a providence and decision about them which is doubtless due to managing the affairs of men.

The quarter is quiet in the toil of its learning, a people in the ebb-tide of tradition, an energy turned intensely upon itself. Big men, some of them walk in robes of fawn, belted at the waist like dressing-gowns, and fur-trimmed hats. Their beards gush in all directions, unbarbered in accordance with Leviticus, and sun-gingered ringlets curl round their ears or dangle like onions in a bistro. But generally they wear black – thin, long coats and wide hats, beneath which the faces are gaunt with the tautness of the ghetto, and the heavy-lidded eyes shine grey or blue. Here and there go the calm features of a philosopher-king, or a dapper, delicate face, reedily boned, passing like pictures or burlesques, Shylocks and Methuselahs. The feeling is of a self-tortured people, bound to its past,

> disposing of everything,
> flesh, mind, the body's rapture of desire.
> Something remains of us, but not ours.
> Often, believe us, it would be sweet to die,
> Not to feel this intolerable pain of history
> to suffer no more for the Name
> written in our eyes . . .
>
> (EMMANUEL LITVINOFF, *Israel*)

But the sects among the Orthodox are many and can only be distinguished by their manner and by differences in dress almost unnoticeably slight. Sometimes they are loosely labelled 'Hasidim', but many are 'Mitnagdim', dour intellectuals from Lithuania who revolted against the eighteenth-century Hasidic mysticism and demanded a return to study. There are the 'Dead Hasidim', who have no religious leader; the 'Gerer Hasidim', who observe a military order and form into ranks for inspection by their rabbi; and the notorious 'Neturei Karta', 'the Guardians of the City', who number only a few hundred and hold that he who transgresses a particle of the Law is lost to eternity. The 'Neturei' throw stones at people who dare to motor in their streets on the Sabbath; they do not recognize the secular state of Israel, refusing to handle its identity cards or money, and it is probably they who spit on the dresses of passing nuns. Their traditional leader, who lives in Brooklyn, curses all those who go to the Wailing Wall before the coming of the Messiah, so the 'Neturei' either never see it or go furtively at night.

It was this joyless legalism, long ago, which caused the Hasidim to draw from the Law a new emphasis. It is a tenet old in Judaism that learning forms goodness, but early in the eighteenth century, in some Ukrainian village, the founder of Hasidism alighted on the text 'the Holy One, blessed be He, requires the heart' (T. Sanhedrin 106. b), and in a few years the ardour for serving God in happiness had spread over eastern Europe. In all things slept the sparks of holiness, the lost divinity in the world, and the humblest man could release them by his consciousness of the divine, by love, by mercy; and in this sacrament of the ordinary his life was transfigured.

So learning no longer kept the gates of paradise, and ignorant man, who is always the majority, felt raised suddenly to the light of heaven, and followed the new path with gratitude. A sense of eternity in the present brought love for everyday things, and helped to give joy in life where joy was little known. Martin Buber describes how a Hasid stood trembling at his window in the early morning and cried: 'A few hours ago it was night and now it is day – God brings up the day!' And if faith, as a later philosopher wrote, 'is nothing but the living consciousness of the Omnipresent' (Leo Baeck, *The Essence of Judaism*), then the Hasid, seeing the form of God in the garments of the world, had awoken to religion.

Such a faith, of course, could not last, and the Hasidim were brought back to a greater respect for the Law. They now study as hard as others, but retain an intimacy in communal life, a custom of singing and dancing, which is wholly attractive. It is they who may be heard shouting at the Wailing Wall in the ecstasy of prayer, and many know a deepened respect for the individual, looking on a neighbour 'as if one wished to come near his reflection in the water and bowed down low to it, and it too comes to meet him until his head touches the water and he sees nothing more, for both have become the one that they really are; so the heart of man comes to man' (Martin Buber, *Hasidism and Modern Man*.

The beauty of this way is corrupted, and the Hasidim have suffered as much as others from narrowness and literalism. Yet I remember walking in Mea Shearim and falling into conversation with a very old Hasid, who looked less like a man than a human waterfall; his beard fell in strands like icicles; his hair, his cheeks, his smoke-blue eyes all drooped in a caricature of ineffable sadness. This is still a city in which one may find oneself discussing sin or the purity of the original soul, and I watched the sudden gladness in him, his lugubrious façade a chance deception.

Finally he exclaimed: 'Come. I must give you a blessing.'

He took me to a room and produced the *tefillin*. He seemed to shiver with happiness. Suddenly I realized that he thought I was a Jew. He found the appropriate prayer in his book and asked me to read.

'I'm afraid I can't read Hebrew,' I said.

He looked surprised, but smiled and answered, 'I will say the words and you can repeat them', and began looping the frontlet over my forehead.

I said stupidly: 'My mother is not a Jew.' What would he say when I admitted that my father was not Jewish either? But already he had realized. He stood motionless, and a flush spread over his porcelain cheeks. The pages of the prayerbook flickered in his hands. For a moment, in my untidy person, he had been poised to release the holiness imprisoned in the world, to reunite the elements of God and harmonize earth and heaven. Now he stared at me as if he had found a stranger in a friend's house.

'Your mother is not a Jew . . . you are not a Jew.'

I could see myself fading in his eyes. The intangible life which two people create had instantly died. Gently he took the frontlet from me and laid it apart.

'But thank you,' I said.

But he only looked at me with his mouth a little open and touched his beard with a slow, Gothic hand. And after I had left I felt that I should have accepted the magic in a foreign blessing, and respected the joy in the old man's soul.

By such simple ways Judaism kept its people in mind of God, and so survived. For Christians its beauty flowed in other channels, and spread beyond the confines which it had set; but they still looked to it as the earliest source of truth. Sublimity, said Coleridge, is

Hebrew by birth; and although the faiths held much in common, the tradition of the past and the vision of the future – the New Jerusalem – belonged first to the Jews.

> And even if our splendour be ruined
> . . . Yet do we hold fast to our crown, the diadem of Thy statutes,
> Until Thou gather our company into the house of Thy choice and Thy desire,
> Our holy place, our glory, where our Fathers praised Thee.
>
> (JUDAH HALEVI)

6

The Mount of Olives

The ancient things have passed away, and lo!
all things are new. The letter recedes, the spirit abounds. The shadows
flee away, and the substance enters.
(ST GREGORY NAZIANZEN)

It is the mystery of the Heavenly Jerusalem that her corner-stone is vanished and nobody may know whether she was founded by the mercy of God or by the desires of lost and fanciful men. The imagination may create according to the needs of the heart, until it is impossible to see how mingled are the cities of earth and heaven.

It is deep in man to love the place where he believes Divinity has walked. To pray there, to tread its earth and touch its stones, may offer him a momentary communion, and the holy sites multiply under his fervour, however light their touch on history. To the Jew, Jerusalem is the symbol of a promise, where his past is sacred and incarnate, and he holds her, if he is religious, in the double bond of his faith and his nation. But Christians see these elements more faintly, and in their place came God himself, formed as a man, his movements so detailed in scripture, his passion so poignant and meaningful, that his steps have been traced in fact or in imagination until they spread in a web of sanctity throughout the city.

To Christians he was more than a prophet; he was the sacrifice of human guilt on the altar of God, the scapegoat which in the older Jewish mystery was led into the desert to die innocent for the sins of others. In this, the mystical tearing of the veil between the Deity and His creation, man is already freed and has only to reach out and accept the open hand of his deliverance. So the person of Christ is the essence of Christianity, and in tracing his steps one finds always a human being, walking in the closeness of history, a man who was by upbringing and in almost all his teaching an orthodox Jew, but whose life and suffering became a part of the world's truth.

A few sites, natural mouldings of land and waters, remain

unchangeable to his memory, and the Mount of Olives is one of these: a low hill to the east, enchanted without beauty, fluted in trampled paths, its foot anointed by the Kidron waters. As early as the reign of Constantine it harboured churches and convents, until the Persians levelled them into the rocks, and time drew the earth over their mosaic floors.

In the Moslem graveyard, as I left the walls, an old man mourned his son in a bitter chant, rolling back and forth upon his knees; and people prayed or walked tensely together, for it was the anniversary of the 1967 war. Along the steep road, where it dipped over the vanished river, Arab women climbed in mourning out of the valley, and standing high above I heard their anguished cry of 'God is great!', pathetic in the stridence of girlish voices, half lost among the flowers and palms held upright in their arms. They climbed from Gethsemane past a mound of stones where Jewish soldiers had died, while in front the police rode their sinuous horses delicately. And looking round, I saw that the valley was alight with sparks of colour, wreaths piled on the white sepulchres, Moslem and Christian, laid where the ancient sages promised life to the slain.

I crossed the Kidron where its valley shines in orchards and the earth rises gently to the east on silted banks. Where the bed of the river has grown hard and high the Virgin Mary was said to have lain in transient sleep before angels lifted her to heaven, and the Byzantines raised a church to her memory early in the fifth century; but it was built, it seems; to accord with suspect traditions, and it is not known whether the Virgin died in Jerusalem or Ephesus. Crusader knights and a Danish queen were buried under its ruined walls, and the Benedictines restored it in 1130, so that Godfrey de Bouillon granted it to them as the Abbey of the Blessed Virgin of the Valley of Jehosaphat. It had the sober handsomeness of most Crusader shrines, and although the upper church was destroyed, the lower one remains, and raises from the river a restrained, harmonious façade whose grey-veined colonettes are grouped discreetly about it and hold up their arches in restfulness and strength.

The passage to the church is greater than its sanctuary – a flood of stairs running through the earth where the blaze of the porch is forgotten. I saw the medieval window to the west, so large that it was said to be a gate, and the funerary chapels of Crusader queens. Of these the early pilgrims spoke, as if no time had passed, and as I descended, the high Crusader strength gave way to something older, the ceilings spread to the calm arch of Byzantium, and I walked in the dark of the church.

Around the tomb's edicule the marble feet of columns were pretty under their grime, where as early as the fifth century the Greeks had adored the sepulchre of the mother of God; and the Crusaders had set it with a gold and silver crown and a band of script saying: 'This is the vale of Jehosaphat, where begins the roadway to the stars. Mary, favoured of God, was buried here, and incorruptible was raised to the skies. Hope of captives, their path, their light, their mother.'

A candle shone in the tomb. I stooped through the groove where a door had swung and passed into the hollow of its chamber, golden and empty. It had been a grave of some sort, cut from the rock around it, now draped in silks; and marble covered the ledge from which the legendary angels had borne the Virgin's body untainted to paradise.

I looked back to the apex of the church and saw its lanterns dripping in their hundreds like the tears of the stone. Down its stairs the daylight flowed like a mist, brushing the steps with slips of silvered light. A clock chimed thinly from an empty confessional, and voices murmured above, where a Greek Orthodox priest and a Franciscan talked pleasantly under a vine.

In a little while the priest appeared with candles, beckoned and pointed to a chapel in the eastern walls.

'Here is the tomb of St Joachim and St Anne, the Virgin's parents,' he whispered, and gave me a candle to place there. But this is a recent tradition, and I lit it to the gay Queen Melisende, whose funerary chapel this had been – the daughter, wife and mother of a king, who turned at last to a life of religion, leaving her austere and beautiful psalter to posterity. Around her empty grave the flower-patterns still ran in a banded arc, and the holes remained where its iron grille had been. Other queens and princes were buried in a vault behind the western chapel: Morphia of Melitene, the Armenian wife of Baldwin II, who was crowned in Bethlehem; the mother and half-brother of Bohemond III of Antioch; and his beautiful sister Philippa, whose love affair with a cousin of the Byzantine emperor adorned the *chroniques scandaleuses* of the time. The priest came close to me. The blessed St Joseph, he said, had been entombed in that chapel.

A candle in either hand, he led me through a shaft of tombs to the mouth of a cistern and round dark apses, half turning from time to time and drawing his tapers close, so that his beard seemed to be in flames and the light showed an old and affectionate face. And as he went he deftly lit every candle he could reach until saints and Virgins shone from the walls with a sweet gravity, and a shallow *mihrab* showed where the Moslems sometimes pray – for they too honour the Virgin.

From the church, lying almost in the Kidron, the Mount of Olives begins its steep ascent, and around these unmomentous places – the hill and the halting stream – grew many holy sites; for Christ, say the Gospels, 'went forth with his disciples over the brook Kidron, where was a garden, into which he entered. And they came to a place which was named Gethsemane: and he saith to his disciples, Sit ye here, while I shall pray.'

So Gethsemane – *Gat shemanin*, 'the oil stores' – lay on the lip of the river at the foot of Olivet, and it must have been a garden in the sense which the Arabs know, an enclosed and peaceful orchard. Early in the fourth century the memories of Christ's betrayal and of his prayer were revered by a rock and a ruined grove, but soon after, the place of the betrayal had become a grotto – now a Franciscan chapel, skylit through a sudden dome.

Sometimes at evening, returned from preaching in Jerusalem, Christ walked over the hill to the house of Lazarus at Bethany; but often on warm nights he slept and prayed with his disciples in the olive-groves, and 'Judas knew the place: because Jesus had often resorted thither' (John 18:2). The slopes are still musky with olives – the tree, wrote Pliny, which never dies – and the Franciscans keep a tiny garden where marguerites and hollyhocks are banked in a massed, devotional jumble, and butterflies, sucking the scented hearts, lightly move ecstatic wings. In the fifteenth century its eight olive trees were already old, and they are, perhaps, the shoots from those which Christ knew, whose trunks were cut down nineteen hundred years ago by Titus, leaving the country round the city bare. Bowed in the mass of their years, they seem not trees at all but the sinews of some silenus sleeping in the ground, bleached and rotted, hollow to the tap of a hand, but rough with the majesty of the very old. The boles which seem dead put out new branches, tufted with silver, spear-headed leaves, where birds sing; and they still bear fruit in summer.

The Byzantines built a church close by in the reign of Theodosius, on the place where they believed Christ to have prayed in agony. Etheria, who came on pilgrimage soon after, described it as 'graceful', and recorded that the faithful, on the night of Good Friday, wended down to it from the place of the Ascension. 'On account of the great number of people in the crowd, who are wearied owing to the vigils and weak through the daily fasts, and because they have so great a hill to descend, they come very slowly with hymns to Gethsemane . . . There is so great a moaning and groaning of all the people, together with weeping, that their lamentation may be heard perhaps as far as the city.'

The church was ruined, like so much else, by the Persians in 614, and the Crusaders spread a new shrine above it, whose apses and walls have left their dissolution in the rock. Centuries later the Franciscans obtained the gardens called the Flowery Field, where the aged olives stand, and where beneath the wrecked Crusader shrine the fragments of the Byzantine church lay unknown. In 1920 while building a new basilica, there came to light a frescoed angel's face with the arc of his broken wing; and the monks found the wraith of Etheria's 'gracefulness': tinkling ghosts of beautiful wall *tesserae*, and shattered floors.

In recent years the Italian architect Antonio Barluzzi has raised on these foundations a smaller church in early Roman style, long and low and triple-aisled on six enormous columns. The rock of Christ's agony has been enshrined as the Byzantines knew it in tradition, lying across the nave to the east, and the floor mosaics follow, where they can, the patterns which still show. So many countries gave gifts towards the building of this Basilica of the Agony that it has come to be known as the Church of All Nations, and across its pediment nostalgic figures depict in rich mosaic the sufferings of the world. The alabaster windows scarcely let in light, but through their moods of mauve and clouded peach a twilight sadness comes, distilling all it touches to a glimmer of foreboding, the awful softness of a grove at night.

I walked here with a friend on the evening of the Betrayal before Easter, descending to the garden from the Sion Gate by the tombs of the King's Dale. The Kidron spoke in the darkness, and between black trees the lanterns of Anglican pilgrims moved through moonlight to Gethsemane. The basilica shed a radiance so soft and mesmeric that it seemed we walked in a Venetian painting, in the half-imagined colours of the agony of the God-man. Beneath the cupolas the coats-of-arms of many nations glittered without vanity, lost in the greater mystery of the church, yet every object held its own translucence, like a well-cut jewel. Pilgrims, kneeling with candles, sang a hushed, antiphonal hymn, and over the moon-whitened paths of the garden the younger branches of the olive trees stirred out of their withered immortality, and the night drew a fragrance from the flowers.

Christ, say the Gospels, withdrew a little from his three close disciples, and prayed to his Father that if it were possible this cup might pass from him, 'and his sweat was as it were great drops of blood falling down to the ground. And when he rose up from prayer, and was come to his disciples, he found them sleeping for sorrow' (Luke 22:44, 45). Behind the Basilica of the Agony the rock remains where they are believed to have slept, and where three times Christ returned to wake them, until Judas came through the grove with the servants of the high priests, and drawing near in the safety of friendship, kissed him.

A few steps north of the basilica the old track climbed to the Ascension, and another now mounts steep nearby, past convent walls. It goes by a second church, hallowing no special site but enjoying the nearness of many – completed in 1888 by Czar Alexander III in remembrance of his mother, and named from her patron saint St Mary Magdalene.

A novice closed its iron gates behind, and left me alone on a terrace, looking to the city where it leant towards me over the eastern crest. Below, the old paths dwindled, traversed by every age, where Christ had walked to Bethany and where David had fled barefoot from a rebellious city, mourning for Absalom.

Dense and possessive on its hills, in Christ's time a lineament of Roman order had showed: the rim of a theatre or a spray of columns; and flat-roofed houses – beams and plaster – were turned in, windowless, upon their courts. 'A hole in the corner', scoffed Cicero, who never saw the city; but soon afterwards Hecataeus of Abdera estimated the population to stand at a hundred and twenty thousand, and Pliny called her 'the most famous city not only of Judea but of the whole East'.

The hills were dark with trees then: ilex and tamarisk, and the hardier fruits and vines, and to their feet the rock-cut stairs went down from many gates. Walls looped west from Ophel, humouring the whim of the slopes, and excluded the watershed of the Tyropoeon valley to mount the western ridge where the houses of the rich stood, and the Herodian towers of the procurator's palace. From their turrets, whose elegance would soon be burnt away, the mercenary sentry looked down upon the lower city, 'the shape of a moon when she is horned' (Josephus, *Wars of the Jews* IV.i), and saw the wooded slopes around me, remembering perhaps his own Numidian forest or the mild plains of Gaul.

The Temple was new, not yet complete but, like a snowy hillock, was heaped upon itself in tiers round columned courts where the priests went barefoot through the water and blood of sacrifice, and caught dysentery; and a stench of burning sickened the upper suburbs on an eastern wind.

This was the familiar world of Christ, the city in whose ambience he moved with grief and understanding and which he saw, despite itself, as his own: a place of little luxury, though the trades of the east passed through it, whose streets were clean not from civic pride but in ritual purity. The people too were careful in their persons, though it was a jape of Roman comedy that the Jews smelt like pigs, and the women wore the ornaments of Bedouin, scented in cassia and lily with hennaed hands and nails, and eyes circled dark in *kohl*. At evening the city closed its gates and the peasants went from the orchards, moving like the centuries, with their hoes over their shoulders in a stooped, habitual quiet. The watch-fires fluttered on the Phasael and the night brought its scented lull, measured by the watches of the sentinels on the Antonia, ghosts in moonlit armour.

The places in Jerusalem where Christ may have trod, owing their truth not to faith but to history, are few and almost ignored. In the garden of the Russian church the rock-cut stair remains which led over the Mount: a fragment only, a broad stone stairway lost under sea-green trees, pine needles thick on the shallow steps no longer climbed.

The Russian nuns move stiffly here and there, exiles and very old, all dressed in black, with conical fur hats. The priests are archaic and slow. The fir trees creak. The church lifts a bundle of onion turrets from a yellowish, cluttered body, and is romantic in a Muscovite way, with mellow, urgent bells. But inside it is Victorian, with a heavy iconostasis (painted by Vereshaguine) and pastel murals depicting the life of St Mary Magdalene.

The Scottish Mother Superior is a visionary who found a balanced way of work and contemplation in the Orthodox church. Her helper, Mother Barbara, whose father had been the greatest banker in Moscow, was in the Kremlin as a child when insurgents killed the Grand Duke Serge whose wife had organized the building of their church. After the murder of the royal family, the body of the Grand Duchess was found by the White army, carried to Peking by a monk and taken by sea to the Holy Land, where it was laid as she had wished in the crypt of the church in Gethsemane. Her portrait hangs in the Mother's salon – she is dressed in white nun's habit – and there are other figures in the room too, saints and Grand Dukes staring from ikons and photographs through dusky, Slavic eyes.

I found a White Russian general living nearby, a handsome, fine-mannered man whose white hair flowed down to a military beard. Aide-de-camp once to Czar Nicholas II, he had brought the remnant of the Imperial Cossack Guard into Yugoslavia when the war was lost, and there they had worked on the railways for a while before disbanding forever. A liturgical reader now, he chanted in the church with the nuns, and looked after his delicate wife with masculine gentleness.

'The past is finished,' he said smiling. 'Why dwell on these things? They are fifty years away, and all our lives have happened in between. In heaven I will not say "I was a general to the Czar of all the Russias"; I will tell them that I was a reader here in the church of St Mary Magdalene.'

He bent near to catch my answer, for he was almost deaf, and I shouted approval.

'To tell the truth,' he said, 'I am not much proud of my youth. But luckily one forgets. Now we are just two old people ending our lives. We are content and we look to God.' He smiled at his wife, as if their happiness were a secret. 'So you are a writer? Have you heard our Christmas services? They, at least, are worth writing of. But don't speak of our past: nobody is interested in that any more. Only say, if you like, that you heard an old man singing in the Russian church at Gethsemane.'

If he should read this, I hope he will forgive me.

Easter vespers are beautiful here, but are like a trance or mourning in the tender sadness of Slavonic chant. The sunlight dies and leaves the church its golden richness, candles clustered before ikons, and the sisters standing frailly in the shadows of their past. They sing plaintive lines which cease abruptly like breaking waves, a longing which expects no answer. A young celebrant stands in vestments of silver-white, over whose chasteness a high crown shines, lavish on the youthful head. 'Christ has risen!' comes the whispered cry; the chant is breathless, a heart panting, the flowing of incense upward. 'Christ has risen!' An old man stands erect and sings melodiously. The nuns cross themselves. And the people – there are three of us – bow and murmur 'Christ has risen!' as we are blessed, and step out of that lost Byzantine glory into the empty dusk.

The footsteps of Christ fade as the Mount of Olives rises. The sites grow vaguer, the tracks spray out, and the villages of Bethany and Bethphage, lodged on the eastern slopes, are no longer in their ancient places. Yet the search continues, with little more than tradition to guide it, and the way leads high above St Mary Magdalene's to the church of Dominus Flevit, 'the Lord Wept'. Shaped like a Prussian helmet, it has a poor, artificial look, not built in the strength of its materials. A low altar and an arched window are the genius of the place – a *coup de théâtre* of Barluzzi – for they enshrine the whole city lying beyond, and commemorate the first Palm Sunday when Jesus rode over Olivet and 'beheld the city, and wept over it, saying, if thou hadst known, even thou, at least in this thy day, the things which belong unto thy peace! but now they are hid from thine eyes' (Luke 19:41, 42).

I saw Palm Sunday commemorated by Roman Catholics in a pilgrimage to Jerusalem from the village of Bethphage. At the head two Moslem guards, ancient and hugely ceremonial, dressed in frayed, embroidered blue and trailing sabres, planted their silver staves in a slow tread: relies of the Ottoman Empire. Acolytes raised a startling gold cross, and behind them, faintly singing, the huge procession unwound itself from the lunar softness of the Judean wilderness. The nuns passed in their hundreds in all designs of black and white – it is said that even God does not know how many orders He has – with brown-clad Franciscan nuns, the nurse-like Soeurs de Sion, Sisters of Charity in blue, the starched white Sisters of St Mary. Their schoolchildren whispered and sang in disordered files and everyone carried a palm branch.

They trailed like a feathered serpent over the spring hills. A cluster of genial, peasant faces showed where the Franciscans trampled a river of dust; the Latin Patriarch and his bishops followed, magenta and purple mingling without pomp, and Moslems trudged after them in an old reverence for Christ. By mid-afternoon they had crested Olivet, and had moved down singing to Jerusalem beyond, as into some air-built tableau, the glassy beauty of Mantegna's city.

Lauda Jerusalem Dominium
Lauda Deum tuum Sion Hosanna . . .

They descended into the valley until the Kidron, from height to height, was looped in a filament of moving palms, and passed through the walls at the Gate of St Stephen while the last monks were still far away beneath the pines of St Mary Magdalene.

Wherever Jesus wept in that first procession, the church of Dominus Flevit holds the city more beautifully in view than anywhere. I met a Neapolitan professor there – a dapper, old-fashioned liberal who scorned modern architecture and could scarcely bring himself to enter the church.

'It is imitative,' he cried. 'It has no *spirito*. Anyone could build such a thing. You put some blocks together here and here and here' – his immaculate fingers let drop an imaginary row of stones – 'and you say you have a building. But you have not. You have a goulash.'

A monastery was here in the fifth century, a happy, domestic place it seems, with a few small columns, and floors patterned in fruit and birds. A mosaic-coated wine-press is complete nearby, where two monks sat in the warmth of their beards, barefoot, and looked ready to leap in and tread out grapes.

'*Mio figlio,*' whispered the professor. 'Regard these mosaics. They were made well, cut of good stone. All modern architecture is *finito* because it employs poor materials. How can you make a good meal out of rotten eggs?' He went on to denounce, in an Anglo-Italian patois, the urbanity of Israeli society, the decadence of the West and the lapse of tradition everywhere. The biblical prophecies of destruction, he added darkly, were coming true, and he walked into the modern chapel as if going to his execution.

The Crusaders raised a church also, and the Turks a mosque, both almost gone. Then, piece by piece, the Franciscans bought the property, and discovered Jebusite graves and tombs tucked together in the rock, which yielded first-century Christian sarcophagi, with lamps and shreds of jewellery. Ossuaries were found, wrought simply in soft stone, inscribed with crosses and names familiar to scripture – Mary, Jesus, Lazarus – so carefully protected in the earth that they are still smooth and weakly painted.

Over the southern hill the modern Jewish graves are washed up like whitened bones, reaching to the Kidron and the Mount of Offence. They rest in simple cubes among thistles, their inscribed, round-headed stones once looking toward Jerusalem, now wrested askew so that inscriptions lie tumbled where no graves are, and other tombs are nameless. The cemetery lay untended for twenty years. A road was run through it and Arabs broke up the stones until the thorns pressed over their desecration and engulfed it. A man is there to help those who search, with a list of fifty-four thousand sepulchres. When one is identified, the family of the dead descend in charabancs from the New City, and their chants and moaning fill the valley. I saw a party of Hasidim resanctify a grave high on Olivet, grouped round it with a conversational ease, their doyen spreading out his arms while he prayed, as the father of a family presides at table.

A German Jew was walking where the tombs were tilted like wrecks in the waves of the grass, but he had seen nothing he remembered. 'It lay north of a four-tiered grave. My father. I recall it clearly. Seven graves north. It has to be here.' The sun had set his face aflame, and the sweat leaked gleaming from the cask of his chest. 'Seven graves north. I cannot find anything. I never counted the rows. If only I had counted the rows. Everything is gone.'

He kept swearing that he remembered the place, but his eyes, pausing nowhere, betrayed a fear that he had made a mistake. 'It must be here. The dome of the Aqsa Mosque was always level with the tip of the wall when I stood by it. The ground cannot have altered.' He looked across the ocean of grass-sown tombs. 'Can it?'

I could not answer him. He might traverse those slopes for ever. We sat in silence, gazing at the city in whose echo the hill is set, and the grasshoppers lisped soullessly round us. I remembered a verse from the Hebrew daily Amidah, that God will keep His faith to those who sleep in the dust; but while I groped for the German words the man moved off. 'Seven graves north . . .' and the sound of his feet died away on the path.

I lay in the weight of the sun. On the wall behind me an insect came glittering, fourteen legs in an undulant flow, and stopped from time to time to wring its hands, as flies do. I wondered how old in grief were these hills, where Jewish families had returned from Babylon and counted graves to the north, and found nothing. I saw another necropolis not far above – the Tombs of the Prophets, of unknown age, where pious Jews locate the graves of Haggai, Malachi and Zachariah. And higher still was the grave of an unknown woman whom Christians identify as St Pelagia and the Jews as the prophetess Huldah, and go through a strange penance, squeezing themselves between the wall and the sarcophagus for the absolution of their sins.

The site of old Bethphage is lost, but the new village has a church and a painted Crusader plinth from which Christ was said to have mounted the ass which he rode to Jerusalem. A track goes in the coolness of trees to Bethany on ageless, polished stones. There is an ancient 'Tomb of Lazarus' and a church to commemorate his return from the dead, built by Barluzzi in the style of a sepulchre, whose windowed dome spills in the light, and holds rich acoustics.

I came there toward evening. A Franciscan with a florid, uncomplicated face sat alone at a harmonium. I wandered about the aisle and saw the flotsam of earlier churches, and medieval buttresses nearby. Suddenly it seemed as if a whole choir was chanting to organs, a vast and beautiful ceremony proceeding behind closed doors, the stones singing. The monk sat at his harmonium, his mouth scarcely opened. I looked around for other people, for some electrical contrivance, but there was only this monastic Caruso, who gazed abstractedly as if with a faint wonder at the glory which rose from him, filling the dome where doves of resurrection flew on light.

Near Bethany, wrote St Luke, Christ blessed his disciples, and parting from them, was lifted to heaven. The village lay higher on the hillside then, and almost at the crest of Olivet the empress Helena, mother of Constantine, built the first church on the hill and called it Eleona from the Hebrew for Mount Olives, where it consecrated the site of the Ascension. Handsome once, with a sleek-columned porch leading to a high sanctuary, there is little left but a musical name. Mosaics are dulled in a thicket to the south, and a few capitals sit above a cistern which the villagers still use. The crypt is half scooped from rock, with a new altar and a cave of tombs below; and legend says that Christ returned there after he foretold the Temple's ruin, 'and as he sat upon the mount of Olives, the disciples came unto him privately, saying, Tell us, when shall these things be? and what shall be the sign of thy coming, and of the end of the world?' (Matthew 24:3). And he warned them of the future, foretelling their death, of the rise of false prophets, the hatred of nations and the love which grows cold.

The ruined chancel has been paved for another church, dedicated by Pope Pius XI after the First World War to 'Peace among Nations and Peoples'. But its building, like that peace, remains a dream, and only a half-wall circles gauntly the place where it should have been, and fir trees are planted down its aisles in a mockery of columns.

To the east, where the Crusaders had raised a basilica to commemorate the Lord's Prayer, an eccentric Italian woman, the Princesse de la Tour d'Auvergne, awaited the Last Day in a chalet which she brought with her from France. She built another 'Pater

Noster' church in 1872, which is white and cool and has a simple cloister copied with *spirito* from the Campo Santa at Pisa. Around it the Lord's Prayer is inscribed in forty-five languages – even Esperanto and Samaritan – on majolica tiles with flowered borders, and when completed the princess gave the building to the Carmelite Sisters, who live in the adjoining convent, and prepared a tomb for herself near the cloister.

The steepness of Olivet eased away. Houses stood along the summit, and men drowsed with their donkeys under trees and watched me curiously. To the north, down the gutters of the hills, goats and sheep trickled together into the valley, and I could hear the anger in the shepherds' shouting half a mile away, and see the circles of their arms as they threw invisible stones.

As early as 387 a Roman lady built an octagonal church called Imbomon, 'Upon the Hill', where monks and nuns were settled as the place of the Ascension. Galleries of marble columns ran inside and a tiled roof lightly covered them, open to the sky above the place of his ascending. At night a giant lantern shone, hoisted on pulleys, and others hung in the arcades, so bright in their glass shutters that they lit the rock-hewn stairway to the valley and even tinted the city. The chapel was a place of miracle. The ground, wrote the Gallic bishop Arculf, was unused to bearing anything human and 'would reject whatever was placed upon it, throwing back the marble into the faces of the men who were laying it'. On its floor the imprint of the feet of Christ remained in the dust, although pilgrims took the earth away with them, and a tempest blew yearly on the day of the Ascension, throwing the congregation on its face.

Then the whole Mount was spread with corn and barley, and was rich in churches which have left their bright mosaics on the hill. The bodies of saints were buried in innumerable shrines, and their heads, fingers and hair scattered about the reliquaries of the empire. By the sixth century the hillside was littered with caves and shacks where hermits chanted and babbled, baleful with foreboding or meek from prayer. They squatted on trees or rocks, and from every hole iconic eyes glared out, an emaciated fist banged its calabash, a voice croaked for charity.

After the Persian sack in 614 more than a thousand bodies were found upon the Mount, but the abbot Modestus rebuilt many shrines, including the Ascension, and hermits were still living on the summit when the Crusaders came. Once more the crumbling sanctuaries rose in splendour. The Ascension was fortified with towers, where a watch was kept by night for Saracens, and its chapel is still elegant on the hill-crest. It has been rebuilt, but keeps a modest grace, its blind arcades looped round an octagon on little blue-veined columns. Marble griffins clash their chests on its capitals, their legs and wings bunched awkwardly about them, and stone-coloured lizards scuttle through its crevices or stare at one another with passionless eyes.

Yet its lightness is transient. In its outer walls Crusader columns have left only their bases, like stone petals, orphaned and mysterious, and the dome was raised heavily by Arabs long afterwards. Since the time of Saladin the Moslems have owned the place, venerating Christ, and have built a small mosque nearby.

The footprint of Christ is no longer traced in dust as the ancients knew it, but is marked in the rock-floor of the shrine – a floor raised artificially, I think, above the Mount – worn shapeless by the touch of pious men. These memories grow naturally out of the Semitic mind: the spoor of feet and fingers on the stone, bodies which do not wither, trees which never die. The Arabs say that the mountains are interlaced with tunnels which link all sacred places. The plants listen. The rocks speak. There is no rationale to these beliefs – they are a manner of worship; and there may be many sites for one event, but all will be holy.

Late in the nineteenth century, on the true summit of the Mount, the Russians built a Church of the Ascension and a hospice among pines: but entry is rarely granted. It is a huge compound, whose priests go tiredly about the duties of serfs, and the White Russian nuns – more than fifty – are stooped and wasted. Over this exiled race the Abbess Tamara presides – she was once the Grand Duchess Tatiana, Princess Bagration – and the services are still beautiful: the ghost of Holy Russia passing away.

The buildings stand on ground already holy, and the nuns see in the red-veined pavement of their church the blood of martyrs slain in 614. In its wall is a stone where the Virgin Mary watched her son as he ascended, and pavements show in a smaller church where the

Armenian convent of St John the Precursor may have stood in the fourth century. An enigmatic dent, confided a nun, had cradled the head of the Baptist, and many mosaic birds, enchanting and natural, came to light under the carpets when I turned them back, where an inscription in Armenian reads: 'This is the tomb of the blessed Susanna, the mother of Artabanus, September 18th.'

I watched the nuns returning from Vespers, nodding one to another with the ease of long friendship. One of them handed me a giant key, lifting it with both hands to mine. She said something in Russian, and smiled in her wintry eyes, turning away from the evening wind and leaving me with a means of entry to a place which I did not know. But looking around, I saw that only the campanile could merit this key. Taller than anything in the landscape, the Ottomans suspected it as a signal tower for spies, but from far away it is pointed and fragile, a pencil which writes on cloud.

I had scarcely mounted its first storey before all Olivet lay in sight: the village of Et-Tur and the Viri Galilei church in its gardens, where columns lie. Beyond was the Augusta Victoria Hospital, raised on land given as a silver wedding present to Kaiser Wilhem and his wife in 1906 and built, it was suspected, as a government house in anticipation of the Germans conquering Palestine. The Kaiser himself was spread in mural over the chapel ceiling, robed as a Greek emperor, but it became the government house of Britain instead, and is doing penance for its imperial past as a hospital for Palestine refugees, cruelly bombed in 1967. Beyond it, north and west, curves Mount Scopus, for nineteen years an Israeli enclave in Jordanian land, whose soldiers were relieved by convoy once a week. From a distance the ruined buildings of the old Hebrew University and Hadassah Hospital seem intact among their cypresses, and the graves of Allied soldiers killed in the First World War stretch in ranks beyond.

The wind roared in the tower as I climbed, beating through the arches where baby pigeons nestled against shelves in the inner walls and watched me sleepily. It was suddenly cold with evening. Far below, the Russian crosses clustered white on the graves of the dying order. So long ago had anyone climbed here that birds had laid eggs in their nests on the stairs, and my feet across the landings left their prints in level dust. I climbed the upper steps where Cyclopean bells hung, dragged from Haifa by Russian women in the days when Moslems feared their chiming as the sound of *djinns*; and reached the topmost balcony.

The wind tore at my eyes and seemed to rock the tower. Yet beneath, the world slept. Circles of sculptured slopes, like thighs and shoulders, flowed one against the next to vapid deserts, touching the northern Negev and the Dead Sea, a sliver of steel. Their crests lifted to whitened tips, all life wrung out, and the Moab ranges were ghosts and emanations of the sky, its dream of hills.

The cones of Herod's palace-tomb shone beyond Bethlehem. In the north the Jordan ran under empty mounds to the orchards of Jericho, which Antony once gave in love to Cleopatra. Far to the west Jerusalem glittered in fragments through a desert wind and by the chance sorcery of sand and evening claimed perfection, the peace and innocence which were never hers.

7
The Passion

The more a man loves, the more he suffers. The sum of
possible grief for each soul is in proportion to its perfection.
(FRÉDÉRIC AMIEL)

Mount Sion carries the upper city on wide shoulders to the south, divided from the hill of Ophel where it outreaches the ramparts and drops into Gehenna. On the spur outside the walls tradition has set many of Christ's sufferings, his appearance before Caiaphas and the betrayal of Peter. But the sites have little to support their claims.

The wind throws the sand idly from ruin to ruin, and goats roam over great heaps of emptiness – that deepest of all voids where once-fervent life has vanished. I walked where the houses had been broken to dust on the edge of the slopes, surrounded by the usual refrain of rubble and wan flowers, and listened to a donkey's misery, foolish and laboured far below. Christian cemeteries were all about the hillock, their iron gates cut by shrapnel, their graves cracked, and it was strange to walk between the high walls where a few months before it would have been death to go.

I traced the traditional route along which Christ was brought from Gethsemane by the soldiers of the Sanhedrin, who 'led him away to Annas first; for he was father-in-law to Caiaphas, which was the high priest that same year' (John 18:13). The Armenians keep a 'House of Annas' on Sion within the walls, where in Christ's time the terraced houses of the rich had stood in cleansing winds. It is attended by widows who sit in its courtyards indifferent as shadows, and is a thirteenth-century church, enshrining a tradition younger than itself, but handsome beneath its gilt, with narrow, domeless aisles. A stone in the chapel walls, they say, bears the imprint of Christ's arms as he was scourged, and would have cried out in horror had not the disciples whispered to it that their Master was divine. The widow who keeps the keys lives nearby, behind the olive tree to which he was said to have been bound, and as she goes in and out of her house she familiarly touches this sympathetic stone.

The records of Christ's trial are confused, and scholars no longer see in them the malice of the Jews so much as the peremptory judgment of Rome. He was condemned, it seems, not as a religious blasphemer but as a political liability, for the fatal name Messiah. By Jewish law the Sanhedrin could not assemble at night; the trial which the Gospels record in the house of the high priest could have been held only by Caiaphas and his inner council, puppets of Rome.

Yet before his arrest Christ might at any time have kept silence or moved to some quieter city on the farther side of Jordan. His passion was voluntary; the Gospels say that he saw clearly everything which lay before him, that after his terror in Gethsemane he went serenely on the way which he had chosen, and gave himself to his executioners as a man whose spirit was beyond their power. For a while he remained a well of silence in their anger, incorruptible and subtly remote, as if the Supreme Good of Plato had been clothed as a man, and Caiaphas, bringing false witnesses, could only condemn him by an honest question. Was he the Son of God?

As early as the fourth century the palace of Caiaphas was shown as a ruin on the ridge of Sion, and the Byzantines set a church to St Peter there, where pilgrims used to pray on the night of Holy Thursday. Years afterwards it fell into ruin, and the Armenians spread their Convent of St Saviour above it, a fifteenth-century oratory which contained many relics. Along its weed-tufted pavements chunks of columns lie, and in the cold of a ruined cloister the tombstones of bishops show worn names underfoot. On one side the little oratory stands, its gilt and fresco fallen in heaps and its tiles splintered round it, while across the balconies I saw the sandbags of Israeli snipers piled together, facing the Sion Gate. Down all the walls the bullet holes were neat and angry, as if a steel wind had blown them, and in the court, where black snakes slept, the baroque headstones of the Armenian patriarchs had been heaved from their oval catafalques in a sad and magnificent confusion.

The hill seemed consecrated again to grief, patient and empty. I found a bleached mosaic under wild passion-flowers – a part of the first church, built to consecrate the trial of Jesus and the betrayal of Peter. More than a church, it was a symbol of God's grace and the failure of man, for in this gift of Himself to the world, the Christians saw their hope. By His own pain God had annulled man's sin. Already the New Jerusalem was built on earth for those who would enter her. Christ, unlike the Pharisees, went voluntarily to men to teach them, and was gracious above all to sinners. To the old plea of Samuel, 'Speak Lord, for Thy servant heareth', he had answered with the new promise to man in his spirit: 'Behold, I stand at the door, and knock: if any man hear my voice, and open the door, I will come in to him . . .' (Revelation 3:20). His sufferings obsessed early Christendom. They were the sinews of its faith, and the holy places which commemorated them made more solid man's claim to salvation.

Many other sites were sanctified on the southern tip of Sion, although it lay outside the city in the time of Christ, and I passed, without knowing, the shrines of David's burial and the Last Supper. Wandering into ruins by walls which dripped with candle-grease under crushed and smoke-blackened ceilings, I thought that I had found an abandoned chapel. But it was a memorial to the Jewish dead of the Nazi concentration-camps – so many that only the names of their villages could be recorded, engraved on panels fastened to the walls. The rooms were almost bare, but filled by the intangible, by horror without the dignity of grief, and a feeling of unforgiveness. Wherever I went the candles guttered in loneliness and stretched megalomaniac shadows about me; and I found the ashes of the murdered on an altar, with gas pellets preserved from the death chambers, and soap from Jewish bodies, as if these could reflect the unimaginable waste of life, the dead who are too many to be remembered.

I stepped into the sunlight again and walked between cemeteries and the masts of pine trees, wind-turned towards Moab. I felt faintly sick. A little girl followed me, balancing a basket on her head, with two onions and a baby chicken in it.

'Do you want to see the Virgin Mary?' she asked.

I said that I did.

She led me by a thin track. A man came on his donkey jerkily, guiding it through the rubble as Nehemiah had, and it turned a winking, dispirited face to me as it passed.

'Hurry, hurry,' said the girl.

'Why?' I asked. 'Is the Virgin Mary going away?'

She lifted her face to mine and from underneath her brows two vast and serious eyes reproved me.

'Virgin Mary does not move,' she said. 'She's in there.'

Beyond her pointing hand the cone of the Dormition Abbey rose secretive and turreted – a Romanesque donjon built by Germans early in the century where Byzantine legend had placed the *Dormitio*, or the Falling Asleep, of the Virgin.

'The Mother of Jesus is in heaven,' I told the little girl piously.

'She's not. She's in there,' came the stout reply.

I found no vestige of age when I entered, but trod in a bare magnificence of stone, a great hall copied from the palace-chapel of Charlemagne at Aix-la-Chapelle, but empty and godless, as if I were walking through the skeleton of some superb, extinguished creature. The starred floor, the altar of dark Westphalian marble, the high, gaunt apse spoke only of the irrecoverability of the Romanesque, the failure to feel again as others felt, to build with the thoughts which are no longer ours. On the barbaric Nordic stone an Abyssinian woman knelt, her quivering hands outstretched in a rhythm of prayer and ecstasy, and bowed her body to the marble.

A statue of the Virgin lay in the crypt and depressed me, until a light voice whispered, 'That's Virgin Mary.'

With her onions and chicken scooped up in her dress, the little girl had crept in behind.

'She's asleep.'

'That's a statue.'

'Ssh.'

'Did the attendant see you come in with that chicken?'

'Ssh. Ssh.' Her eyes grew wide with worry. She thought that the statue was going to wake up.

I took her by the hand and hurried her across the great aisle where she skated in dirty sandals like an insect on a glazed pool.

'Why? Why?' she kept asking.

'Because people have to get permission to come in. And they don't allow chickens in church.'

'Who don't?'

'The people who live here. Benedictine monks.'

'It's a small chicken.'

We crept out under the disgusted gaze of a guardian; then the smothered bird was replaced on her head near the onions and she moved away with an exaggerated dignity toward the Sion Gate, turning round on an afterthought to call, 'I told you Virgin Mary lived there.'

I went down the eastern hillside where the last of the churches of Sion stands on a Jewish necropolis, and the slope grows old with rock and eases into valleys. Some five hundred years after Christ the Armenians dedicated a monastery to the Tears of St Peter, and in medieval times it superseded the impoverished 'House of Caiaphas' above, and became the chief sanctuary to St Peter on the hill. But by the fifteenth century even its ruin had gone, and the grotto where the apostle was said to have wept was choked up, so that pilgrims could only remember him by chipping fragments from a boulder.

Eighty years ago the Assumptionist Fathers excavated the remains, and later built a church with the Crusader name of St Peter Gallicantus, 'the Crowing of the Cock'. Wherever I went under the scented trees the grass lapped on sculptured walls, or folded over forms too gentle to be guessed. Chambers and stairs were sunk all around, and here and there a water channel showed or steps led down to dust-floored rooms, where the Jews had laid their dead, and Arabs stabled flocks.

The old church has vanished under the new, but has left itself in patinated clumps of plinth and column, where the mark of chisels two thousand years silent is pale and careful on the tombs. Corinthian capitals are there, well-cut and supple, with poorer Crusader work and patios of white mosaic, betraying a monastery built modestly but well. A pretty bronze lustre was discovered too, the handle of a eucharistic spoon inlaid with stones, some Hebrew weights and a ring engraved with an illustriously feathered cock.

The Assumptionists are sure that they have uncovered the remains of the palace of Caiaphas, and as I wandered about the new church an ascetic young priest came hovering to my elbow. Did I realize, he asked, where I was?

On the remains of ancient Jewish tombs and a Byzantine basilica,

I answered, but he waved these away with a flicker of his petulant hands.

'Look at the church,' he said. (We stood in a sickly fantasy of pastel paint and glass, as if a child's crayon book had been monstrously enlarged.) 'On this place Christ stood before Caiaphas to be judged, and Peter betrayed him. If you follow, I will show you.'

In the crypt the scarp of the hill rose bare. Above it, said the priest, Caiaphas had lived. He spoke quietly, emphatically, but with a faint plea, as if expecting contradiction.

'We are standing now in the courtyard of the High Priest, where Peter sat on the night of Holy Thursday. We do not know exactly where Peter denied Christ,' he added, looking around as if he might soon select a site, 'but across the courtyard we have found a prison, and is it not reasonable to suppose that Christ spent the night there?'

This was the fifth 'Prison of Christ' which I had endured in Jerusalem, and as we descended to a narrow hall, held on piers hacked from the live hill, the priest's tale faded from my consciousness. I grew intrigued by the place for its own sake – a little stable, it seemed, perhaps built by the Crusaders from a Jewish tomb. Rings had been bored in the rock for securing horses. But the priest's voice had grown high and emotional. He was peopling the walls with spidery criminals, chained at the wrists in gymnastic positions to account for the rings. He filled the whole place with groaning and clanking and torture, while I continued to see a friendly troop of tethered horses. Where a pier had fallen from the slight arcades, he resurrected a 'Pillar of Flagellation' and summoned many nameless apostles to be scourged. But the imaginary horses munched their barley disinterestedly, and the priest, suspecting that I did not believe him, pointed to his *pièce de résistance*: two oval troughs in the rock floor.

'We know,' he said, 'that water and vinegar were used in Jewish times to revive scourged prisoners. I think it is only reasonable to suppose that in these two basins . . .'

A ghostly stallion spat out oats.

'And now if you will follow me . . .'

We left the room in darkness, the shrieks and whinnies of our twin imaginations fading away. The last glitter of the sun lay on the floor of the crypt, and we descended again where a group of grizzled Africans knelt in a tomb, their prayer a tempest in its tiny cell. It had served as a cistern later, and in the ceiling a hole was smoothly bored for drawing water; but the priest stood in triumph beneath it, pointing to carved and aged crosses which I could not discern, and a blotch against the wall in which he saw the fresco of a man with praying hands. This, he said, was the prison into which Christ had been cast on that holy night after his arrest.

'The prisoner was lowered,' he whispered, 'through that hole above – how close the scriptures are! – and dropped into the cave.' But I only heard an irreverent splash, and saw buckets travelling amiably up and down its gloom.

The sun had set when we left the church. The whole Jordan valley was aflame beyond Olivet, and swifts dangled in hordes, not knowing where to go, and sank with their wings curved behind them, like black anchors through a carmine sea. Somewhere within the city walls Christ had in truth been taken on that night, when 'Peter followed him afar off unto the high priest's palace, and went in, and sat with the servants, to see the end' (Matthew 26:58).

I thought, despite myself, of evil and denial; of Peter, the archetypal sinner, who saw his greater self deformed in the flame of his conscience, and 'went out, and wept bitterly' (Luke 22:62). The sacrifice of God, sang the psalmist, is a broken spirit; but for deep guilt the Jews prescribed only a communal confession on the Day of Atonement, and devotion again to the Law. It was Christ who said that sinners are loved and that sorrow brings forgiveness as a tree grants shade. So the tears of Peter were accepted, who betrayed his Master and himself, and pain – the eternal price for love and wisdom – gave its promise for the future, and he became the chief of the apostles and the first to take Gentiles into the church.

On Sion the wind had fallen and the clouds had left their tatters in the east. I came to the rustic path which goes down in steps to Siloam, built by the Byzantines perhaps, or by Herod Agrippa II seeking work for the builders no longer employed on the Temple. The stones were laid pleasantly as they were found, half-fitting together, and one cannot tell how old a path they cover, nor who trod before them on the bared earth. Some earlier track, sloped to the upper city, was buried there, had felt the steps of Christ and carried the centuries of eastern maidenhood to the fountain pool below – Abraham's daughter walking easily in the years of her people, with her balanced pitcher and straightened back and the long, free stride which the desert taught.

At Easter the drama of Christ's passion relentlessly quickens, and even the search for his footsteps in the city must cease for a moment while faith bursts into an old and gorgeous ritual. All through Maundy Thursday the churches celebrate the moment at Passover when, in a gesture of simplicity, Christ 'laid aside his garments; and took a towel, and girded himself. After that he poureth water into a basin, and began to wash the disciples' feet . . .' (John 13:4, 5).

Such humility is poorly attuned to the grandeur of the Greek Orthodox Church in Jerusalem, whose Patriarch is all but God on earth. Across the parvis of the Holy Sepulchre acolytes come in salmon-coloured silks, holding a golden cross and the fans from a vanished court ceremonial; censers swing through a foggy redolence, and out of the Church of St James the bishops, vested in gold and purple like Russian fairy-tale kings, process in a hieratic calm, inflated and portentous after the three-hour Liturgy of St Basil.

'Behold,' rises their chanting, 'I was shapen in iniquity; and in sin did my mother conceive me . . .'

The bells pound out a crashing, archaic rhythm, heralds of judgment, and at the church door the Blessed and Holy Patriarch appears, stupendous in a globular Muscovite crown, glittering fat jewels; his beard explodes over dalmatics of gold and scarlet and beneath his jewelled fingers the pastoral stave, crowned with bicephalous serpents, taps its way slowly to a dais carved with little golden angels.

'Do good in thy good pleasure unto Sion, build thou the walls of Jerusalem . . .'

Black-clad women cross themselves in their hundreds, and press photographers cluster round, holding up light-meters to the Patriarchal nose. He sits with his twelve bishops, symbolic of Christ among his apostles, but cushioned in agreeable state like a Byzantine emperor convening ministers. As the Gospel account of the Washing of the Feet is read, he is divested of his more extravagant garments and is girded in a towel, while a golden basin is filled from a silver ewer. The bells have ceased. Franciscans crane perilously over the eternal scaffolding of the Holy Sepulchre. With the aid of four priests, who seem to carry him like a vast teddy bear, the Patriarch arises. 'Wait,' murmurs a deacon. His jewels are rearranged on his chest. His words are held before him in the holy book, and if he loses the place there is always an eager, ecclesiastical finger to discover it. The apostles look nervous and fidget their feet under their robes, and one by one, with god-like solemnity, the Patriarch gives them a desultory wipe.

Other churches follow the same rite. In their chapel above the Holy Sepulchre the Coptic bishop touches with water the foreheads and palms of all his congregation – a simple, happy act, like a blessing – while a child-choir sings. The Abyssinians go through a crumpled ceremony on the roof of St Helena's Chapel, and wash the feet of all the congregation in bay-leaf-scented water.

The Armenians celebrate in the afternoon in their Cathedral of St James, where myriad iridescent lanterns hang, so that the congregation seems to be caught up in the branches of a Christmas tree. A silk curtain is drawn back and shows an altar tapering upwards, chaotic and rich. At its foot twelve bishops and Vartabeds sit in pointed cowls like Spanish penitents, each with a candle and a cross, and appear to be a part of their background, static and mindless in pale, feminine robes. This is a ceremony of muted radiance. The Patriarch dabs the prelates' toes with benevolent detachment, washing only the right foot on which he draws a cross and sprinkles salt for purity, and the apostles remain in their tableau, august and patrician, like a Tinteretto come to life.

The Syrian Orthodox are the last to celebrate, almost at sunset. A rustic, very traditional church, its people in the city number scarcely more than a hundred, and they all cram into the little church of St Mark. Children sleep or shout to each other to be silent, and a choir of boys on a balcony forgets the chant and squeals in Syriac before faltering to silence. Some of the apostles are represented by laymen, and the Patriarch calls out each of them by name from behind a screen, beginning with the eldest, until at the end comes no Judas, but the thirteenth apostle, Matthias – a doe-eyed boy, bland innocence in place of guilt incarnate. The Patriarch, robust and merry, puts off his dalmatics to show a cassock of cardinal red. The apostles stretch out grimy feet with satisfaction, and he flings the towel over his shoulder like a Turkish bath attendant, and scrubs.

Good Friday dawned cloudless as other dawns. Already the Jewish city had been quiet for four days in the Passover. I went down the Via Dolorosa to the Antonia fortress, on whose ruined pavements Christ had been condemned to die almost two thousand years before. There were strongholds here in earlier Jewish times, guarding the Temple in the north-west. Solomon may have built one, and Nehemiah threw up a bastion after the return from Babylon, 'defended by many towers, built to their tops in very large cut stones' (the letter of Aristeas), and the Maccabeans raised the fort Baris on its ruin.

Herod, while he built his Temple, cut the scarp sheer in the north and perched a castle upon it: a complex of massed towers and ramps which he called 'Antonia' in honour of Mark Antony. At the time of the Roman procurators it held a cohort with cavalry. Pilate occupied Herod's apartments, and it remained until Titus captured it by guile in AD 70 and razed it before his assault on the Temple. Years later Hadrian set on its broken courts the eastern archway to his new Jerusalem, and the road which it spanned became the Via Dolorosa, which cuts the old fort in two. On one side the scarp is still high above the Temple area, and keeps its watch on courts of shining calm, the ripe and perfect beauty of the Dome of the Rock. On the other the Sisters of Sion built a convent and a church a hundred years ago, where Pilate's judgment court has left its pavements in the hill's strength. Here, where Christ may have been condemned to die, pilgrims venerated his passion as early as Christian pilgrimage is recorded, and although the Citadel has also been regarded as the place of his trial, the claims of the Antonia are more fully developed.

The compound is quiet and ordered, with no demand on the emotions other than the awe of history. The nuns even have an elevator going discreetly up and down its centre, and they take visitors round with a proud matter-of-factness, like housewives showing off their kitchens.

'We enshrined Hadrian's arch in a church by mistake,' a Scottish sister admitted brusquely. 'We thought it went back to Christ's time.'

A serious young nun, taking me to the back of the basilica, pointed where Herod's stones were still enormous in the rock, and with a few gestures rebuilt the castle's archway overhead and slid a lost portcullis down its groove. We descended into guard-rooms, close chambers cut in Herod's day from emptied tombs, and saw the apertures where their fortified doors had swung onto the vanished entrance-tunnel.

'And here,' she said simply, 'Christ walked to his crucifixion.'

At our feet was a ramp of stones striated in brutal ridges to make firm the hooves of horses. Laid where the entrance thrust into the fort, the stride of cohorts had cracked and polished them. Over their roughness Christ must have carried his cross. The grave sister was silent, but obscurely must have loathed the mindless stone, the material Roman heart which all but crushed the gentleness of its time.

In Herod's storage-rooms, where an aqueduct from the Quarries of Solomon came sheer through the rock's heart, we passed in the silt a stone shot from the mangonels of Titus. From the palace level we descended again by Roman steps and into darkness. The walls were clammy under my hands and smelt of earth. Somewhere rain dropped invisibly, dying in a vaulted quiet, and far away I heard the sound of praying. Below us in the silence lay a crystal emptiness – water so limpid that I dashed my foot in it before I knew it to be there. The ceilings of a cistern stretched vast and rounded to darkness, stones so beautifully laid that not one had fallen since they were built by Herod. Its limestone blocks were graded for their hardness, Roman and secure, and could have held the subtle waters for ever. As the piers sloped down, their arched reflections rose to meet them through the pool, touching unseen, and echoes sang in other cisterns, far away.

All this Christ would not have known, but went into the courtyard while the Jewish priests, who would not defile themselves by entering the house of a Gentile, clustered outside and accused him. Pilate, bemused by the silence of the gentle prophet, offered to free him as the Passover gift to the people. But the crowd, say the Gospels, cried for the life of a murderer in exchange, and 'when

Pilate saw that he could prevail nothing, but that rather a tumult was made, he took water, and washed his hands before the multitude, saying, I am innocent of the blood of this just person: see ye to it. Then answered all the people, and said, His blood be on us, and on our children' (Matthew 27:24, 25).

But this Roman pity and open weakness no longer go unquestioned by scholars; Pilate, like most of the procurators after him, was a military man, proud and vicious, unbending to Jewish demands, and history has not so freely washed his hands of blood. It was probably in the courtyard of the Antonia that his sentence was pronounced – 'the hall called Praetorium' (Mark 15:16), where Christ was mocked and led away to die. Round the court a peristyle ran unadorned and a few walls and pillars have traced its course, with lamp-sockets, plinths and capitals of the glossy *acanthus mollis*, speaking a faded strength, without delicacy. St Helen, said legend, carried its stairs to Rome, and Pope Sixtus V laid them by the chapel of the popes as the 'Scala Santa', where those who climb must go upon their knees.

In the judgment-hall the pavement, the *Lithostrotos*, is left – a part of Pilate's court laid bare. I stepped there as if on glass, almost afraid: a flood of many-tinted stones, fiercely broken where the upper ramparts crashed upon them; and even the nuns walked delicately, as if they might waken spirits.

'And Jesus stood before the governor: and the governor asked him, Art thou the King of the Jews? . . . Hearest thou not how many things they witness against thee? . . . he brought Jesus forth, and sat down in the judgment seat in a place that is called the Pavement . . . and he saith unto the Jews, Behold your king!' (Matthew 27:11, 13; John 19:13, 14).

The paving-stones are huge and ugly with years, some of them six feet long and hewn from beds of the hard *mezzy* limestone, which has grown a marmoreal polish on its wrinkles. Their colours pass through every shade of stone, shell pinks and travertine and alabaster, with here and there a line of champagne-tinted blocks, grooved to guide the rain away to cisterns.

We stooped under vaults whose piers showed votive plaques, and the nun pointed downwards. There in the paving I saw the games with which the Roman garrison had idled away hours off duty – a light-cut web of stars, circles and squares, like the paths of insects. There were hopscotch rectangles, where knucklebones were thrown – 'to win', wrote Ovid, 'a man must cast three pieces in a straight line' – and other dice were slid to tiny troughs still dimpled in the stone: games which Arab children play in the streets.

I saw a spiked crown and the letter B, carved on the flagstones for the *Basilinda*, the Game of the King. This was a harmless play of dice, but was a variant of the Saturnalia, that free and sinister festival so popular in Rome; sometimes the legions would elect a mock ruler and allow him to vent his pleasure until he was killed in mime, and it has been suggested that the soldiers, turning from burlesque to reality, used Christ as the puppet-king when they clothed him in purple and a crown of thorns.

Yet most of these *lusoriae tabulae* are mysterious, and tell only of the Roman passion for gambling; of the ordinary moments of bored peasants far from home; of the lazy stream of life down simple channels. Year after year, between the judgment of Christ and the aborted trial of St Paul, the knucklebones tumbled into their grooves, skating across the stones as trivia play across the surface of everyday, the thousand pauses which are the tissue of life.

It was natural that the Romans should condemn Christ as a Messiah. He had not quarrelled with the Jewish Law but with those who professed to follow it. 'The scribes and the Pharisees sit in Moses' seat: all therefore whatsoever they bid you observe, that observe and do; but do not ye after their works: for they say, and do not' (Matthew 23:2, 3). He preached the religion of the heart and its intentions – 'for the letter killeth, but the spirit giveth life' (II Corinthians 3:6) – and above the tyrannous skein of rules he put the first and great commandment, reminding the people of their most ancient laws, the truth which they had forgotten. His words were not framed for synagogue debate, but echo Galilee, the vigour and simplicity of peasants. With understanding he saw evil, by perfect vision knew good. Above all he asked for love, which alone could purify the response of man to his world and his God.

His was a cleansing, liberating thought and nowhere better than in Jerusalem may one see the breadth of his following. From the rustic devotion of Franciscans it reaches to the scholarly piety of Dominicans; from the mysticism of Russian Orthodox to the rationalist sang-froid of the Soeurs de Sion; from the supine faith of Greek Orthodox to the impassioned self-effacement of the Little Sisters of Jesus. Even in the convent where I lived, the temperament of everyone was different. La Grande was not so much a nun as an elemental benevolence, robust and effervescent; Gentle Sister had the qualities of St Francis, Laughing Sister the virtues of St Clare; and Madonna kept a tenderness of her own, coupled surprisingly with a certain authority when she knew what was right, so that love and justice seemed aptly balanced.

These sisters, in different ways, reflected the passive virtues in Christianity. They never missed a day at the Holy Sepulchre. Early in the morning their faint hymns reached my room, and sunset would find them in their chapel with their prayer-books on their knees. But there was a member of the order, Sister Rafaella, who confounded anybody's preconception of a nun. She was the active element in Christianity, organizing, feeling, fighting. When the Orthodox Jews spat at her in the streets, she considered what was best for them, then spat back. Her whole person was an assertion of life, radiant and sure. On the others the world's evil seemed to fall powerless, so calm was their faith; but injustice drew from Sister Rafaella a sickened, incandescent anger. She remembered the Second World War in Poland, though she appeared too young, and she could never again, she said, look indifferently on pain. All this was clear in features of piercing, almost masculine beauty, a broad-boned, aristocratic face out of whose pale complexion the hazel-green eyes glittered startlingly.

In the 1967 war she abandoned the shelter of the convent cellar and went out into the streets during the fighting. She emerged among the Israeli pickets on the Via Dolorosa before they had time to shoot, and ran into the French hospital, where a handful of nurses were trying to save a multitude of wounded. At mid-afternoon they took the dead to St Stephen's Gate and buried them in mass graves in the Moslem cemetery, where low stone monuments cover them.

After the war Sister Rafaella began to collect orphan girls from the streets. She found an empty house on the Mount of Olives and there they had remained, with whatever clothes and furniture they could beg. Sometimes they came for a morning to the hospice – ten little girls in a medley of donated frocks. They reminded me of schoolchildren anywhere: one vivacious and feminine, who would normally have been spoilt; a dark, serious hoyden; and a knock-kneed child who was always the last. But like many Arab children they gave an impression of eyes wandering about on legs. Often it is as if the face first grew from the eyes, which begin life large and luminous; but later the bones press up like sorrows beneath the flesh and the vision withers away.

'We are here to *act*,' said Sister Rafaella. 'These children will never know a proper home if we let them go. They are still mentally ill. One saw her father dead and woke up screaming twenty times a night for months. She had to be fed piece by piece like an animal. Another still keeps saying that her father is in Kuwait. And another was disordered and used to wander about pointing to angels in the air. She scared everybody.'

She laughed suddenly with a buoyant humour which was never far from her. 'This orphanage will be our life now. So long as one crust of bread remains, and one glass of water, we will be here.'

It was the genius of the sisters that they had made this pocket of loss and emptiness happy and half-secure. The children sang and danced in the evening – sometimes Polish dances, whose Slavic vigour was too great for their undernourished legs, which spurted out desperately beneath them until they fell over. But Arabic dances they knew naturally, moving in circles around the serious girl who steered them round with her deep sable eyes, while Always-the-Last sang a nasal desert chant and beat out the time incompetently on a tin mug.

While the state school taught them to be useful, the sisters taught them to be happy, but there was a slightly illicit look to their ragged contentment, suggesting a flock of cherubim mingled with the urchin pickpockets from *Oliver Twist*. And when they glided in a wavering crocodile through the bazaars, they did not belong there, but seemed like the spirit of Jerusalem in her self-inflicted sadness, the walking conscience and failure of man.

The Eastern and Western churches celebrate Holy Week separately and it is incidental if their dates coincide. The pilgrimage of Roman Catholics up the Via Dolorosa, the traditional route of Christ to

Calvary, is special to their Good Friday. Only their starting-point at the site of the Antonia fortress, and their end at the Church of the Holy Sepulchre, may be valid in history, but this old and beautiful Way of Sorrows is the flavour and memorial of pilgrimage itself – the last of the journeys which must still be made on foot.

In Byzantine years Christ's march was already remembered in a night walk from Gethsemane to Calvary, but its precise itinerary is lost. Throughout Crusader times the present way was followed by the Templars and Augustinians, and was developed in the fourteenth century by the Franciscans, in whose care it has remained. Pilgrims began to form sacred ways in Europe on the pattern of what they had seen, and as these became more elaborate, the Via Dolorosa itself began to conform to them, and was lined with sites which were sanctified only in tradition. Three hundred years ago the Way had almost found its present form, with fourteen stations clustered along it, but it lay already sixteen feet above the Roman city level.

Pilgrims used to start from the Crusader chapel of the Repose on the Antonia ruins in the south, but when I came on the morning of Good Friday, I found that the little chapel had been shaken down by an earthquake long before, leaving only a sheikh's tomb which the Turks had laid inside it. The Mamelukes had taken its columns and placed them in a minaret nearby, and their capitals hold figures of Christ and comforting angels, worn to wraiths.

The tradition that Christ was here crowned with thorns has almost vanished, and has become attached instead to a sanctuary in the Franciscan Biblical School on the Via Dolorosa below. Its cloistered garden is scattered with fallen columns. On one side is the façade of the Chapel of the Condemnation and Imposition of the Cross; on the other the darkened profile of the shrine of Flagellation and the Crowning with Thorns.

The Western church, which has always emphasized the Passion, has been assiduous in erecting these memorials to suffering. The Flagellation was built by Barluzzi on Crusader ruins and is a russet, sentimental shrine incorporating a twelfth-century gargoyle of two amiable bovine heads. The Condemnation rests on part of the paving of Pilate's judgment-hall, which spreads unhallowed into the convent's lapidary museum, stacked with the pristine ossuaries from the Dominus Flevit. A passage goes beneath it by a heavy, enigmatic ramp, and through the darkness, like the clash of tiny cymbals, the rain can be heard dripping into the pools of Herod.

Here, by the Chapel of Condemnation where the steps of the 'Scala Santa' are supposed to have run down to the castle court, pilgrims venerate the Second Station of the Cross, and the crowds on Good Friday, descending slowly from the scarp of Bethesda and into the street, knelt and prayed and went by in murmuring throngs.

Soon they had filled the eastern road and had passed the Orthodox 'Prison of Christ' where ghoulish red lights hang in Hasmonean tombs. Beyond, a chapel had been built out of Mameluke baths where tradition claims that Christ fell under his cross, and there they knelt in the dust again to pray, and moved on slowly south. They bore huge wooden crosses on their shoulders, the men jostling to hold or touch them, and their hymns were curtained by the streets, as a wind brings and takes away faint sounds, so that in one moment the hymns of French pilgrims had vanished under a reedy Anglican chanting, and in the next, this too was gone before a rush of Castilian voices from portly, sensuous women.

Mira, ingrato pecador,
Perdon, oh Dios mio!

They passed the Fourth Station of the Cross, where the Virgin is claimed to have met Christ and fainted, and where the Armenian Catholic cathedral of Our Lady of the Spasm stands. In its crypt mosaics from some older church show two delicate yellow sandals traced in *tesserae*, precise and mysterious, like the tread of an assertive goblin.

The pilgrims turned west where the way climbs long and steep by tiers of steps – a sad and beautiful street in the medieval imagination – with little vaulted shops and cafés, and houses holding many strands of age. Donkeys mince under sacks of grain, their leaders' faces dusted with flour, and pass under arches built quaintly between high walls against earthquake; and groomed, effeminate priests stroll up and down.

From the place where Simon of Cyrene helped to carry the cross, the procession reached the Sixth Station, at which St Veronica in legend wiped with a cool cloth the sweating face of Christ, and received on it his everlasting image. The memorial to St Veronica – 'Vera-Icone', 'She of the True Image' – is deep under street level, wedged on the floors of the Byzantine church of SS. Cosmas and Damianos, where waves of medieval arches break darkly above a chapel of stone and iron.

They climbed in black flocks, a thousand people carrying the cross which one man had borne.

Pro peccatis suae gentis
Vidit Jesum in tormentis
Et flagellis subditum.

The voices were weaker now, the people sweating; few knelt to pray. At the Seventh Station, where the city wall had been, Christ fell again, and in Hadrian's day some monument had marked a crossroad of the *Cardo Maximus*, and has left its column in the Latin chapel. By the Greek convent of St Charalambos, Christ spoke to the women about him: 'Daughters of Jerusalem, weep not for me . . .', and the sacred way leaves at last its ripple of steps, and enters the Church of the Holy Sepulchre under the clash of bells.

8

The Church of the Resurrection

I am the Resurrection and the Life.
(JESUS CHRIST)

As a child I imagined that death was planned to fit harmoniously into God's scheme of life. Yet it forced me to realize that the world did not rest in the hands of adults, and even heaven seemed too poignant a change from the friendly human state. Paradise and hell were drastic, medieval places, strange with skeletons and angels; and these, with several other childhood fantasies, have never entirely lost their grace and terror.

More than any other building, the Church of the Holy Sepulchre resurrects these thoughts, for it enshrines the traditional sites of both Calvary and the empty tomb, the loss and the triumph, the mighty seeming-opposites of darkness and light. Hell and heaven return as gentle irritants, ghosts which come back to haunt the daylit house of the mind. More than a church, it is a microcosm of eastern Christianity, sleepy and sensuous when it is not fervid and disputatious, but for many a living evidence of salvation.

The debate on the site of the Holy Sepulchre has given birth to a whole literature. It was an old contention that it lay within the walls of Christ's time – it is far within the walls today – and that because burials by law took place outside the city, the tomb must be false. But now it is known that early in the first century the land around the church was countryside, and that the ramparts – the elusive 'Second Wall' of Josephus – excluded it in their jagged climb from the Antonia fortress to the Citadel of Herod.

The Gospels say that Christ was crucified in 'the place Golgotha, which is, being interpreted, the place of a skull' (Mark 15:22), and that 'the sepulchre was nigh at hand' (John 19:42). As a warning to passers-by executions were usually held by a road or outside a gate, where the upright of the gibbet remained standing so that only the crossbeam need be carried by the condemned on his last walk.

Christ's crucifixion – probably in April, AD 30 – seems to have passed unrecorded in its time, for it was doubtless assumed that no more would be heard of his teaching.

In the three centuries which elapsed between his death and the conversion of Constantine, no word of the sepulchre or of Calvary is known. The growing city smothered the place where the Church of the Holy Sepulchre stands, and soon after, Jerusalem was obliterated by Titus. The Christians fled beyond Jordan and the date of their return is unknown. In 135 Hadrian covered the future holy site with a forum and temples, and almost two hundred years went by before Rome became Christian. Then, writes Eusebius in his unctuous *Life of Constantine*, the emperor ordered excavation on a site which appears to have been venerated in tradition, and 'beneath the covering of earth, appeared, immediately, and contrary to all expectation, the venerable and hallowed monument of our Saviour's resurrection'.

Ancient historians wrote later that Constantine's mother, Helena, 'being divinely directed by dreams' (Socrates Scholasticus, *c.* 420), journeyed to Jerusalem and discovered the holy cross, which was identified by being placed on the corpse in a passing funeral, and 'wonderful to tell, while all stood trembling, the dead body was shaken off, and stood up in the midst' (S. Severus, *c.* 400). A part of the cross remained in Jerusalem and a part was enclosed in the emperor's statue at Constantinople, while the holy nails were forged as a bridle for his horse in war, and mounted as a crest upon his helmet.

The discoveries of Helena may have been organized by the ecclesiastics of Jerusalem to humour the empress or to raise the prestige of their city; or perhaps they were arranged as propaganda for an empire whose members were still mostly pagan. But the location of the site by Constantine is significant – the belief that the holy sepulchre lay under Hadrian's temple to Venus, far within the city walls. The old topography of Jerusalem would have been forgotten by then, and in the search for a likely tomb the bishops would have selected a site outside the ramparts of their time unless tradition had told them otherwise.

Or did they have shallower motives? Was the site chosen spitefully to overthrow the pagan sanctuary? Or arbitrarily set near the spreading forum, where a great church could conveniently be built? Or did they merely guess, and choose by chance a place which archaeology would honour? There are no answers, and this site, the most significant in the belief of the world, has kept its enigma, the suspicion that the truth was, after all, nurtured through those three centuries, and that pilgrims tread here on the place where Christ was crucified and buried.

Constantine's church was beautiful, the most rich and sacred of his day, but is all but lost: a dream-form anchored on a few walls and arches. The triple entranceway, it seems, was cut in the ramparts of the 'Second Wall' built by Herod or the later Hasmoneans, and the columns of Hadrian were used again by Constantine and set in a portico before its steps. These giant foundations rest in the Russian Hospice Alexandre east of the present basilica, and spread incongruously through a neighbouring confectioner's shop. Beyond them, the atrium of Constantine once lay porticoed under sunshine, and worshippers ascended many steps to wash at its pool. Deep in five aisles of amber-coloured stone, they moved through the Martyrion as ants through harvest fields, and saw above, lifted on shining columns from the dark, the interlacing roofs of sculptured gold.

'I have no greater care than to splendidly adorn this holy place,' wrote Constantine, 'that not only the church may be more beautiful than all others but that even its details may excel those of any city in the empire' (Eusebius, *Life of Constantine*). Beyond the Martyrion, the hummock of Calvary was hewn from the slopes around it and set with a jewelled cross; and a courtyard led to the holy tomb, cut from the rock and clothed in the rotunda of the Anastasis, whose dome, 'the crown of all the building' hung lightly on an arc of silvered columns.

For three hundred years the pilgrims trod its halls in peace, but in 614 the Persians sacked the city, and Modestus, after they had gone, was barely able to restore the church's frame, whose decorations would never again know the richness of Constantine. Four centuries later the mad Egyptian caliph Hakim wrecked the sanctuary, 'destroying the holy tomb even to the last vestige' (Yahia of Antioch, *Annals*), and the emperor Monomachus could only rebuild the Rotunda and raise an oratory on Calvary, leaving the Martyrion in ghost-like glades, where its fallen columns were plucked away.

But in 1149, fifty years after their capture of Jerusalem, the Crusaders consecrated a new church on the old. They raised on piers a monumental choir with high, unequal transepts, enfolding all that was sacred in a towering harmony. Its entrance lay no longer in the east, where it drew an ambulatory round traditional shrines, but was pierced in the southern façade.

In spite of fire and earthquake, and restorations more disfiguring, it is the gaunt and lovely genius of the Crusader church which still stands over Calvary. Shops and sanctuaries hang on its flanks, and for almost as long as can be remembered the southern façade has been shored up in iron. But underneath, its stones break into ripples of fastidious moulding, and the restored Crusader cupola perches tapering on its drum, like the domes of Aquitaine.

The courtyard was empty when I entered and only the stubble of a portico showed across its paving, crinkled and shone by tides of pilgrim feet. The church looked more ancient than its years, sunken and defensive where older chapels pressed their walls on its court: the Greek Orthodox St James', with eighteenth-century ikons and medieval door; the domeless pendentives of St John's, the shrine of Forty Martyrs under the headless belfry; the Greek convent of Holy Abraham and a tiny Armenian chapel framed in the apse of the vanished St Mary Latina.

The front of the mother-church lay captive between them, half-seen for thirty years behind scaffolding, but showing the firm, exquisite richness of the Romanesque in its fruition. So subtly does its style remember Rome that the cornice from some Hadrianic building was set on an eastern window, and the mouldings took their mood from it, fluent and sure. The double gateway is handsome, with dentil moulding heavy on its arches and the columns in marble clusters, their capitals accomplished with a masculine fineness, but it has been half blocked since Saladin's time and there are empty spaces where the tympana used to be.

In the imponderable flowing of Romanesque into Gothic, even the lintels, taken temporarily to the Palestine Archaeological Museum, place the façade in the older tradition. The western panel portrays the raising of Lazarus, Palm Sunday and the Last Supper: not living scenes but mystical expressions. Linear robes flow down from tensed, unhappy faces, and here and there a figure may still be known – the smashed head of St John resting awkwardly on the Master's withered hand, Lazarus drawn empty-visaged from the tomb – for emotion is in the body's movement, the faces only mists with formal beards and transfixed eyes. The eastern panel is more subtle and extraordinary, and carries a giant plant, a Tree of Life perhaps, in whose whirling mythic birds and people swim – harpies and eagles with trottered feet, a centaur clutching a ready bow – entangled in symbolic dance.

In Crusader years the Patriarch could enter the church by a western gate still immured in Christian Street, and the shrine of Calvary was reached by steps ascending from the court, and through a hall above them. This has become the Chapel of Our Lady of Sorrows, and the stairway remains by which the knights went up to Calvary, with the vestibule elegant and complete, its dome nestled against higher walls. Climbing to where a pillar stood uncrowned, I saw the weathered beauty of its arches. Two bearded monkeys held hands on a cornice, and stone birds hid in the drip of sculptured leaves, showing only their feet and lightly moulded wings.

For years pilgrims were plunged in the church's veneration. Twilit stairs and tunnels linked a cipher of chapels, shimmering El Dorados heaped about each other; gaunt saints gestured out of a frescoed gloom, and in the sunless ambulatory went becalmed, archaic faces. The feeling is still of a factory or museum of faith: the lair of the Eastern church, ruled not by aesthetic order but by the religious dance of the liturgy. Orthodox, Copts and Armenians inhabit its sanctuaries happily and screen themselves away from one another, loading their shrines with an opulence which numbs and dazzles its worshippers into subjection. Their ambience is the flickering flame, the initiate sign, tradition and glory; its forms elaborate, its mind intuitive.

But in the last few years the main religious sects have agreed on restorations, and now the high, near-Gothic beauty of the church is growing again out of its tumult. In the great nave the Greek priests blink in an unaccustomed light. A Western cathedral stands luminous, a pale twelfth-century giant which for all the dark imaginings of its time is attentive to the loveliness of form. Everywhere its stones are new and plain, but the old blocks and capitals have been used where they can be, the medieval lines discovered. Lightly broken arches reach airily from clustered piers, and columned windows are sunlit in the dome's drum. Over the transepts sweep the thin-ribbed vaults, conceived long ago in England, by which the church passes lightly from the Romanesque to the Gothic.

The new stone is of the soft *malaky* used by Constantine and brought from Kalandia where the Romans had a quarry. The restoration is hundreds of years overdue. Twice the Franciscans undertook repairs, and after the fire of 1808 the Greeks restored the church with every blunder in construction and taste. The conch-shell apse of their choir shows a baroque triviality and a Crusader pilgrim would no longer recognize the Rotunda. They busied themselves in deleting most of the Roman Catholic structures, and d'Aubigny's grave only survived by chance, forgotten under a bench where Ottoman soldiers sat. The cenotaphs of the great Crusaders, Godfrey de Bouillon and Baldwin I, had lain for seven hundred years below Calvary, where Chateaubriand was the last to describe them; for these too the Greeks demolished, and only their inscriptions are remembered: Godfrey, they said simply, 'conquered the whole of this country for the Christian religion' and 'King Baldwin, the second Judas Maccabaeus, hope of his country, vigour of the church, strength of both, to whom Kedar and Egypt, Dan and the murderous Damascus brought in trembling their gifts and their tributes, O sorrow, lies in this narrow tomb.'

In 1927 an earthquake brought the church to the verge of collapse, and Britain volunteered to repair it, but the religious communities wrangled, then refused. For over thirty years it has been braced in scaffolding. Not until 1959 was agreement reached, but the main work may soon be finished. Among its architects of all denominations, a learned Dominican father is engaged in a study which is overturning many earlier conceptions of the building. He is more like a faun than a monk – a tiny, nimble man with eyes of pagan mischief and a jovial sprout of beard.

'The fourth century church is everywhere here, more than anyone at first believed,' he said, pointing to rounded arches west of the transept. He had thrown off his white robes to reveal a little boiler suit, in which he climbed all over the building and high onto the scaffolding of the façade, from which I sometimes glimpsed him leaning like a friendly gargoyle. The church offered him total delight. The more complex it became, the happier he grew. He darted up ladders and gambolled among debris, and took no notice when lumps of falling masonry exploded at his feet.

'But I have lost my *feu intérieur*,' he complained, vaulting a pile of planks. 'Ten years ago, why . . .'

Beneath our feet, as we entered, was the grave of Philip d'Aubigny, governor of Jersey and tutor to Henry III; on the west the divan of the Moslem caretaker to whose family the keys were entrusted by Saladin. Several guides clutched at me and whispered of the places of Christ's suffering: the slab of polished limestone where his body was anointed; the wrought-iron canopy near which, Armenians say, the Holy Women watched the Crucifixion.

On my right the hill of Golgotha was locked in walls fourteen feet high, holding the shrine of Calvary. The Romans cleared its earth and trimmed the rock, and I climbed where rotted pillars were sunk to their necks in the floor and the stairs dwindled to a vaulted glimmer under the mosaic legend *Ubi Crucifixerunt Eum*. The shrine was small, shared by Greeks and Roman Catholics, and through its columns half the church showed. In the Greek aisle a priest drowsed; in the Latin a woman knelt alone. I stood between their sanctuaries as if beside two avenues of thought. Mosaics glistened over the Latin vaults and stretched to an altar given by Ferdinand de Medici in 1588 and set with copper panels of the Passion. But on the walls were narratives of death – the Holy Women mourning, the sacrifice of Isaac – and behind its cross the Virgin rose in jet-black above Christ Crucified: not a gentle, grieving mother but a pallid Fury.

The Franciscans keep an altar nearby, where they suppose the Virgin to have watched the Crucifixion. A young man knelt before it with his hands spread out and stared up mawkishly at the two hundred-years-old Mater Dolorosa: a statue painted and carved from wood in Portugal so skilfully that it appeared to be of plaster. Her marbled eyes were coy and alive in the candlelight. About her hung the nearly priceless gifts of European princes; her heart was pierced by a sword of sorrow, her head starred with a gold and diamond halo.

The chapel proclaimed the Latin reverence for the Passion, the afflicted body of the Man of Sorrows, dying Son and wounded mother. But in the Greek aisle all was cluttered glory, the ceilings so low that the plunging of lanterns and the upsurge of candelabra clashed in a glistening curtain. Frescoed figures swarmed darkly over the vaults, leaving the sheen of their haloes and armour bodiless, faces and robes half washed away in stars and cherub wings. Gifts from Greece, an ebullient Russian chandelier, candlesticks given by Kaiser Wilhelm in his customary bad taste, a golden picture from Czar Nicholas II, all trumpeted the kingdom of Christ, who hung crucified over the altar in a rain of gold, painless and triumphant.

Two nuns knelt to kiss the silver-rimmed hole where they say the cross was set, and placed their candles tenderly in its darkness. The sites were all pointed out bluffly by a priest. Black discs showed where the crosses of the thieves were set, and a gash in the rock was exposed for veneration; for as he died 'the earth did quake, and the rocks rent; and the graves were opened; and many bodies of the saints which slept arose . . .' (Matthew 27:51, 52).

It is the Orthodox way to invest the Crucifixion with victory, while the Latins see it in greater isolation; but for each the death of Christ is a penance before a betrayed God. He has become both magistrate and victim, suffering Himself the punishment which His justice demanded. In the vaulting above me, its *tesserae* even and sure among the poor mosaic round it, Christ Pantocrator was portrayed in the last fragment of Crusader decoration. His was a face of judgment, starved and censorious, his hand upraised in an obliterated blessing, garments billowing to spectral feet.

The Christian does not claim the status of the Jew, who stands before God in the strength of his piety and may acquire merit in the face of the Divine. But in the Crucifixion, in the mystical sacrifice of innocence to death, sin lost its power. It is the measure of this God's love that He suffered not only the physical torment of the *supplicium servile*, the Roman slave's death, but separation from His heavenly essence, from the God who seemed to have forsaken Him.

Christians believe that He came as a shepherd to His sheep, to lead but not to drive them. They have only to follow; and because He liberated them, their relationship is not merely the service of mortals to some cosmic deity, but a personal affinity of confidence and love.

I descended by steep stairs, drooping as if the gilt and worship hung upon me, and was glad to pass into the ambulatory away from the demand for reverence. Beneath Calvary a shrine consecrates the myth that Christ was crucified above the grave of Adam and that the blood flowed down in absolution upon the head of the first man. After the plea of Calvary it was pleasant to rest in its shabbiness, where two stone benches casually marked the graves of Godfrey de Bouillon and Baldwin I. Nobody ever worships here, since Adam is not favoured, but I dropped a coin, as the custom is, onto the split rock where he was supposed to have lain.

The Greek Orthodox keep their treasury nearby, but to gain access to it is as tortuous as canvassing an audience with the Grand Turk. Bishops and archimandrites take refuge behind arcane and vaguely benignant smiles, and mumble the names of metropolitans and archbishops who must first be consulted and who in turn, after many days and many messages between the Patriarchate and the summer palace, pass on the almost invariable refusal of His Beatitude. But the treasury is one of the most luxurious in the world, filled with gifts from Greece, Constantinople and Russia, worked mostly in the last three centuries, vestments from Vienna, embroidery of Georgia, chalices, crosses, Gospels, reliquaries, mitres, 'caps of humility' and every kind of liturgical instrument, sometimes more rich than beautiful; the sword of Peter the Great which a pope gave; and pieces from the 'True Cross' enclosed in a crystal reliquary for the emperor Heraclius, and in a ruby- and diamond-studded crucifix decorated in the last years of the Paleologi.

I heard Franciscans chanting in the Rotunda, responses to a prayer which distance drowned, and schoolchildren followed them from Calvary, their voices exalted in the softness of a hidden organ. From the underground Chapel of St Helena the hymns of Armenian priests reverberated, and after a while they filed past me, shouting instead of singing, and climbed to Calvary behind the flamboyant bustle of a bishop. In the nave the voices of the Greek Orthodox rose in a whining parrot prayer and from his shrine behind the Holy Tomb came the bawling of a Copt.

For centuries the sects have wrangled. The fury engendered by the running of Latin electricity wires through Armenian property or the sweeping of Coptic dust into a Greek chapel, springs not so much from religious zeal as from a time-dishonoured tribal possessiveness. Six communities divide the church: the Latins – Franciscans – were installed after the Crusades, the Greek Orthodox almost since Christianity began. The Armenians acquired rights in 1829 by their influence in Constantinople, and minor concessions were granted to Copts, Syrian Orthodox and Abyssinians. In Ottoman times the Great Powers entered the lists, France in support of the Latins, Russia for the Orthodox, and in 1852 the Turks reaffirmed their paralysing *Status Quo*, which froze the positions of all the communities in the crumbling church. Only limited restorations were possible, since agreement could never be reached. There were scuffles and knifings round the Holy Sepulchre, and for years Moslem policemen stood guard to prevent the ministers of God attacking one another in the Holy Places.

I climbed through the disused Chapel of St Michael by vast, deformed passages where shreds of plaster and iron hung out like savage fingers, up through the Coptic church of Holy Angels, which the Abyssinians dispute, and onto the roof. So jumbled and interlocked is the hill of shrines that the Coptic convent is difficult to discover, but a youth took me to one of their chapels, thrusting into my hands a notice:

'This is a church Queen Helen.

'This water when Helen take it the water, and Building the church of the Holly Spulecer. This church of Holly place.'

He saw my look of dismay.

'You understand,' he said, 'when Helen come building Seplica water when take it the church Holly place.'

I said I quite understood.

We passed through a door into the blackness of steeply falling steps. Nothing showed but a skein of damp on walls. After a long descent the youth stopped, picked up a tin attached to a string, and lowered it. Far beneath, reflecting our candlelight, the water awoke in golden circles from its darkness, and trembled to extinction. He drew up the brimming tin, dipped his fingers, and touched their coldness to my forehead for a blessing.

'Behind wall on right is Chapel St Helen,' he said. 'We are far-far down.'

There were other 'Cisterns of St Helena', I knew, which lay to the south beneath the church, as old as Constantine, bearing the Greek inscription: 'the voice of the Lord upon the waters'. But I could not see how high or deep was the well in which we stood, for we were misted in our own candlelight with only an intimation of things around, and the walls of the vault might only have been the walls of the dark, I could not tell.

I ascended where the dome of St Helen's Chapel sat gracefully on the waves of its roof, and the arches rose broken and eloquent from the walls, where the Crusader Canons of the Holy Sepulchre had walked in their cloisters on the rooftop. The place was covered in plaster hovels, where Abyssinian monks were sleeping away the afternoon. Four hundred years ago the Abyssinians had a firm tenure in the church, but were ousted little by little until they built their hutches on the roof.

Surprisingly, they live with their women in tiny cells whose entrances are daubed with crosses. Pepper trees drip along the terraces, and a mulberry sheds its purple stains along the pavements. They are dark men with kingly faces, courteous and slow, aristocrats in rags who come from the fortress towns of Gondar and Makalle where the salt caravans go, and descendent, they believe, from Solomon and Sheba.

Their rites are tinted by a *mélange* of hoary cults, and culminate once a year in a haunting ceremony which has been called 'Searching for the Body of Christ'. On the night before Easter I was given a candle as I entered a black and red spotted tent, patterned like a leopard's skin, and sat with a few other guests while the Copts tried to stop the ceremony. I could hear muffled, angry voices. The people in the tent moved uneasily. The year before, the Copts had hurled rocks and many were wounded.

At last the arguing ceased, and the high, mellow bells which had been set in a Crusader window were fervently rung. An almost casual chanting arose in the tent. Drums and cymbals sounded. The priests came in vestments of gold-embroidered scarlet, with banners whose purple cloth fell shredded from golden dragons, and under a parasol lifted regally behind him, the abbot entered. A high crown spangled precious stones in a fringe about his head and framed a submissive face, delicate and young, whose eyes were cast down. The priests sang nasally and hummed as if intent on something within themselves, a mere assertion of being, like a whining of mosquitoes. One by one, the worshippers' candles flickered out. A huge man beat a drum dreamily. Incense left a faint mask on the air and the sistra trembled with silver sounds, as they had once brought purity to the temples of Isis. Everything glittered and flared under the closeness of the tent, but a hint of poverty remained in the creased vestments, and every now and then a monk would enter informally and whisper into the abbot's ear, and he would remain still, his nervous, inbred beauty unruffled. The voices saddened as they remembered the dying Christ, the laying in the tomb, the coming of the women at dawn, until the priests moved out at last into the blackness.

Slowly, as if to exorcise some demon or invoke a mystery, they circled the dome of St Helena, the abbot's parasol high above him in the night wind, the white-robed worshippers behind, searching for the body of Christ, it is said, and bewailing the triumph of death. Three times they circled, in drum beats and the dream of sistra, their candles dim, their shadows lean before them, until they danced like a troop of shining genii, tangled in temple music and the tap of staves.

I wondered, as I walked about the great church, if earlier pilgrims had secretly felt a tinge of disappointment at the shrines which consecrated the death and resurrection of the Christ of Chartres and Burgos and Salisbury. Yet there is little to record it. They appear to have been suffused by the sanctity of the place itself, by ecstasy and absolutions. They jostled to light candles in the Holy Sepulchre as a charm for their pregnant wives, and line the rocks of the Chapel of the Cross with their shaved hair as a cure for headache. In the Chapel of St Helena they heard ghostly splashing from a marble basin in which Pilate was believed to have washed his hands; and beneath the Rotunda a phantom ironmonger hammered nails for the cross. They chipped away surreptitious flakes of holy stone, gathered stray dust into phials and stood with wonder at the 'Centre of the World' – an omphaloid stone which is still in the nave – for here was the axis of the continents where God took clay and fashioned Adam, 'working salvation in the midst of the earth' (Psalm 74:12). In the seventeenth century several hundred Christians slept for months among the dust and fleas of the church. Their servants broughts meal to the gates, which were almost always locked, and the family inside would recognize the intonation of its bell, which hung with a hundred others at the entrance, and would receive the food through a gap in the door.

Where steps go down from the ambulatory to the subterranean Chapel of St Helena, the pilgrims have engraved ranks of tiny crosses, neat and anonymous on the walls. It is a sad, resonant chamber, lost in greenish light, as if its massive columns leant in water. St Helena was said to have watched the discovery of the cross there, and the Crusaders restored the earlier sanctuary, laying huge, blunted capitals on their pillars, and building where the Byzantine walls still grew in a sheen from the rock. A stairway leads to a cistern where the cross and nails were supposed to have been found. It is a shrine now, which bears the unhappy ecclesiastical title of the Chapel of the Invention of the Cross, and holds a plain altar given by the Archduke Maximilian, the tragic emperor of Mexico.

Under the fishbone vaulting of the ambulatory I came to forsaken chapels – no more than apses in the walls – dedicated to St Longinus, the Parting of the Raiment, and the soldiers' insults to Christ; and I walked among the pillars of the northern transept, built as an arcade by the emperor Monomachus, buttressed by the Crusaders and split by fire in 1808. They stand in motley sheafs, Byzantine and medieval – a museum of jumbled shafts and plinths with the bases of columns used wretchedly as capitals. But some remain magnificent, born of the artistic fantasy of Bourgogne or Auvergne. Ebullient capitals show pagan beasts with the bodies of men, peering from whitened leaves like demiurges, ugly and enchanted; and I saw a rustic Merovingian king seated comfortably in a worn acanthus.

At one end of these 'Arches of the Virgin' is an altar to St Mary Magdalene, placed, say the Greeks, where she met the resurrected Christ; at the other is a sanctuary of sunken strength which the Orthodox imagination has dubbed a 'Prison of Jesus'. The Rotunda and the Holy Tomb lie beyond, but I felt unwilling to enter. I wandered into Franciscan domain, where heavy-headed pillars stood immortal in the rubble, set up, it seems, in the time of Charlemagne;

and there was a restored stairway where the Crusaders once entered the church from Christian Street. The little courtyard was intact although its windows on the ambulatory were blocked, and all around were fragments of fourth-century battlements, vaults from Justinian's time and low, heavy-lintelled monastic doors, classically Syrian.

I peered into the sacristy. A marmalade cat was strolling pompously among surplices. I found the silver spurs and pectoral cross which are said, without truth, to have belonged to Godfrey de Bouillon, and saw the dark, serviceable sword whose blade may have been his, used to invest the Knights of St John. At night it clanged on Godfrey's shield in his tent at the approach of danger, and it was said to have leapt alone from its scabbard to attack the unbelievers.

The Franciscans have their conventual church nearby, the ghosts of fourth-century windows still in its walls; and the monks venerate a Column of Flagellation here, a grimy phallic stub against whose shaft they say that Christ was whipped. Numbed by the press of years and the confusion of shrines, I went back into the ambulatory. The Franciscan cat sauntered out, stalked a spider into the Chapel of Insults and was chased by an Orthodox priest. I sat among the burnt pillars and wondered how the preaching among the hills of Galilee had been so transformed, had atrophied into this white magical chaos.

On the evening before Easter I gave the nuns roses, and Gentle Sister made little noises of enchantment, raising her hands at their beauty, before placing them in the chapel. We sat round the courtyard in the mildness which descends with April nights, and La Grande produced a bottle of brandy which a Jesuit, she claimed, had given her.

I listened to monastic sounds – the glug and clink of bottle and glass and murmurs of benediction; and we drank to peace on earth. La Grande grew mellow and expansive and Madonna said that we would all meet again in heaven. 'Life is sometimes hard. There are always wars,' she said, 'and you see that this house is old. The kitchen is low and there are many steps; but because of our hardships we will fly higher in heaven.'

'Certainly,' said La Grande, who did not look as if levitation were her forte. And the others nodded and smiled through brandy-bright eyes. They will doubtless preside in the gold-paved courts of whatever celestial convent is being prepared, where their lives will continue as serenely as on earth. I am sorry that I may not be there to see them.

I went that night to the Blessing of New Fire in the convent of the Dominicans, whom I found in their courtyard, the moonlight skeletal on their pale robes. The bonfire burst to the sky so savagely that the Paschal candle could not at once be lit, and they waited in a circle round its furnace, their faces glacial in the jagged light as if they were burning a heretic.

Then the great candle was dipped to the flames and carried like a column into the church's blackness, touching the pillared aisles to life – the fire of the resurrected Christ in a lost world. A pure solo chant came out of the darkness:

'*Lumen Christi . . .*'

'*Deo gratias . . .*'

The celebrant lit his candle from the deacon's, and the fire multiplied down the long procession in the nave until the lovely Gregorian *Praeconium Paschale* rang softly in a field of golden blades.

'This is the night in which first You led our fathers, sons of Israel, from Egypt, to cross dry-footed over the Red Sea . . .'

The Orthodox, who cling to the Julian calendar, celebrate the Holy Fire at the Sepulchre on the Saturday before Easter, and the flame is symbolic of the resurrected Christ Himself. The ceremony was already established in the ninth century – Bernard the Wise was told that an angel lit the fire on Easter night – and by Crusader times it had become a famous miracle. Even early in this century the crowds were so crushed in the Rotunda that they trod three deep on one another's shoulders, and companies of soldiers were kept under arms to control them. From the courtyard horsemen took the flame to Bethlehem and Nazareth, and it was carried by steamer from Jaffa to the churches of the eastern Mediterranean.

By noon the ambulatory brimmed with people, and the nave was banked in Orthodox priests whose *kalimaikons* bristled jauntily like factory chimneys all awry. Over the massed heads around the Tomb faded banners were parading. I looked at the Rotunda. The slender thrust of Constantinian pillars, the open Pantheon dome, the serene and simple tomb – all these had gone, destroyed by fire in 1808. The arcades, braced in scaffolding for thirty years, were cased in piers so thick that they almost formed a wall. Golden lanterns hung in deserted galleries where the sun fell lifeless, and the painting on the dome flaked down in sordid tassels like a skin rubbing away.

These will, in time, be given back to beauty, for the columns of Constantine still live in the rude piers, and can be restored or copied. But after the fire the Greek Orthodox built around the empty tomb an edicule too solid to offer an excuse for reconstruction – a rococo fantasy crowned with a foolish dome, in which they locked the hopes and faith of Christendom.

The church was in gloom. People clung to the scaffolding and clambered round stairs. The galleries began to fill with consular parties, fidgeting high up like puppets in the incense-thickened light. Shadows passed over the roof of the tomb as clouds touched an invisible sun. The sacred lamp was placed inside, and the entrance sealed again. The hymns and babbling swelled together. The Copts pressed their banners to the front of the procession and scuffled with the Armenians, whose traditional right it is to lead. Flocks of nuns swayed breathless in the crowds.

While the sepulchre remained quiet in the centre of adulation, the Orthodox Patriarch came from the Catholicon and processed three times around it. But as he entered it with an Armenian Vartabed the silence was sudden and utter. The door closed behind them. The crowds stared up to heaven or craned toward the tomb. A minute ticked away. In the mist of the dome a bird flew round and round – a pagan mystery – and we waited in silence for the sign.

Then, like a trumpet: 'Christ is risen!'

'*Risen! Risen! Risen!*'

Two brands flared from the openings of the tomb and leapt through the outstretched candles of the crowd. The bells clanged and boomed like beasts in ecstasy. Sacred parasols sprouted in the air in a trance of drums and cymbals. An Armenian runner bolted past me to his people's chapel with the sacred flame in a lantern, and the Vartabed was hoisted on a chair and carried out of the mob. Already the fire played through the Greek Catholicon and the Copts and Syrians had lit their tapers from the Patriarch's flame.

From candle to candle it ran along the darkness of the transepts and into the galleries. Solemnity had become a carnival as if God was drowning in the ocean of His creation.

Two Russian Orthodox swore that they had seen the fire descending from heaven; but now only smoke rose sleepily to the dome, pierced by a dart of sunlight. In the courtyard, delegations had carried the fire away to other churches and taken it homeward to light the ikons of their saints. Slowly the people in the transepts scattered, holding lanterns of coloured glass or little, gilded lamps, whose fire they passed over their faces – for that which comes from heaven will not harm – until only a tiny woman was left beside me, nurturing a broken candle, and kissed the flame in the gathered darkness.

At evening I went back through the nave where a predatory-looking priest was strolling with an offertory-basin. I came to the entrance of the Tomb, and as I stepped into its hush the bells of the great tower began to chime forbiddingly. I crouched in a tiny vestibule – the Chapel of the Angel – a baroque casket, amber and warm, along whose marble walls were angels; 'for the angel of the Lord descended from heaven, and came and rolled back the stone from the door, and sat upon it' (Matthew 28:2).

I wondered whether to enter that other chamber beyond, and felt, with surprise, the faintest, breathless fear. Something spoke sadly out of my childhood. Had Constantine been right? Was this bizarre shrine the grave of God, who 'turnest man to dust; and sayest, Return ye children of men'? (Psalm 90:3).

I stooped into the chamber. It was like entering a flame or a heart. A throng of lanterns hung there, silver and gold. I felt again the close, baroque oppressiveness. The ravaged tomb was cased in clouded marble, where someone had sprinkled jasmine to form a cross. A black-draped figure slippered in, bent and kissed the stone and cried out suddenly from the heart, vanishing so quickly that she might have been a shadow. I tried to imagine a garden, a country sepulchre, to feel some token for one who died to lift up mortal man to perfect God. But I could not, and went out into the Rotunda. How ugly and empty it was! There must have been flowers and olive trees when the women came with spices at dawn.

Through a low door I found the Syrian chapel, the poorest of all, pitch-black – a bountiful darkness – and held my candle over its abandoned altar. A picture stood in a tarnished frame, behind whose cracked glass I saw a faint folding of hands and robes, and a face of sadness darkened almost to nothing: some lost saint or attribute of God. I groped around the walls, close-vaulted, and my fingers touched a core of well-dressed stones. Curved behind plaster which dripped to tatters, these were the oldest blocks inside the basilica – an arc of chiselled, Constantinian strength – the forgotten apse of the Mother of Churches.

A low door led into an old Jewish sepulchre of a familiar kind: the grave, says legend, of Joseph of Arimathea, who begged Christ's body from Pilate and placed it in 'a sepulchre that was hewn in stone, wherein never man before was laid' (Luke 23:53). The necropolis held two *kokhim* shafts, and others blocked, where the bodies had lain anointed in their shrouds, with ossuaries below. In such a tomb history, not faith, may have placed the body of Christ, but in the candlelight it reflected only my own shadow, grotesque and close: an uncouth place, emptied, I imagine, by thieves instead of angels.

I returned to the Syrian chapel where the arcane picture stood on its altar. Many walls away, the monks were chanting on Calvary and even in this recess a strain of incense crept, the ageless rites continuing. I brushed the dust of the graves from my knees, and passing the altar, left my dying candle to the hallowed unknown.

9
Byzantium

Behold, he put no trust in his servants; and his
angels he charged with folly.
(Job 4:18)

Spring vanished, and in May the *khamseen* came, the desert wind which turns the sky misty and saturnine and leaves a shadow of sand on everything it touches. People grew irritable and sick in its heaviness and the alleys were empty by noon. The pine trees dripped dust, the city glared and dazzled, and summer showed itself in a myriad small things, even in the dazed sleep of the convent cat and the luke-warm water which flopped out of the taps; and butterflies came flying through my window. Later the heat was dry and fine and I felt the clarity of the Judean air – not the diamond quality of Greece, but a dry distinctness which brings its beauty with the shyer tints of dawn and evening.

Sometimes a groaning sounded beyond the Jordan, and aeroplanes went like silver spears to the east. In June there were riots; men threw stones from the battlements of the Damascus Gate and mounted policemen with their long truncheons cantered clumsily up and down Suleiman and Saladin streets, the Arab crowds chanting and scattering around them. Army helicopters whined like giant mosquitoes above the roofs, and I grew as used to them as to the everyday noises under my window: donkeys clopping up and down the steps, the thwack of switches on their raw flanks, and the urging cries of the men as the beasts squeezed their laden bodies through the iron pillars in the alleys; the muezzins' call to prayer, twined melodies dismal and sinister in the night like the pleading of wolves; little boys playing Arabs and Jews with sticks in the streets.

'Bang! Death to the Jews! Charge!'

'*Sssssssh.*'

Jerusalem is a hard city, inured to cruelty. The children are always crying, and are brutal to each other. Animals live cunningly or perish, and even plants struggle. When a person dies it is said that 'Jerusalem killed him'. Often religion brings intolerance, or amounts to no more than incantation, the gaze of the darkened soul on the unknown.

But the toughness of tradition, the possessiveness and pride in Jerusalem's uniqueness are ineradicable. Religion, not commerce, chose her for a great city, and lapped her in the barrenness of the earth, in rock-sown hills and deserts, the stigmata of God. She does not please the senses by bathing them in beauty, nor soothe the mind with the intimation of things not seen, but sharpens it by problems and resurrects old tensions. Indifference is not possible. Her people and buildings are the children of beliefs. Religion and politics forever touch hands, and whatever happens to Jerusalem is trumpeted about the rest of the world, while equal events in other cities go unheard. Symbol and lodestar, 'a city that is set on an hill cannot be hid', and in the declarations of Arab and Jew one clause is constant: neither is prepared to give up Jerusalem.

Sometimes I caught glimpses of the haunted tableaux which Holman Hunt saw when he walked through the *sugs* a hundred years ago: the stance of a woman, perhaps, in the gloom of medieval walls, a merchant's gesture – verses of the Bible scattered in alleys. But the woman bargains harshly and the man spits. Scripture is clothed in its proper dress – the Semitic world unchanged at its heart.

Already by July the grass had paled, and the corn shimmered high and green in the valleys of Ephraim where the women bent over ripening crops, as Ruth had worked in the sight of Boaz. The nuns in my hospice came from the rich, sugar-growing fields of western Poland, and the aridity and heat upset them. Even the canaries ceased to sing. But the lemon trees in the courtyard showed their fruit – tiny, green urns with a hard, bright glaze – and the canna lily unfurled a crimson banner. The convent routine grew quieter. Gentle Sister padded remotely about her business, her feet wrapped in huge socks, like a panda. She fed me on Polish *bas cuisine*, so vast and varied that each meal was a landscape – a hill of batter scallops tufted with *golomki* meat balls, ranges of spiced sausages, a cascade of eggs, salads and strawberries; all this was set before me matter-of-factly month after month, although a consistory of cardinals could not have finished it.

La Grande was boisterously concerned for me. She had been in Jerusalem more than half her life, and had only once, after thirty years, returned to Poland, to find her aged sister; but she was miserable that my parents might be lonely without me, and gave me presents of writing paper. My clothes were starched like the nuns' head-dresses, so that shirts could be battered into shape like Gothic armour, and underwear made genial crinkling sounds. She scrutinized my face for signs of illness. When I rubbed my eyes she pressed dark glasses on me, and seeing me walk barefoot in the courtyard, she marched into the heat to buy me shoes, coming back jubilant with a pair of Japanese sandals. When I pointed out that one was white and the other yellow, she shook with laughter and bellowed: 'It's better than having one white and the other red!'

I began to discover the nuns' individuality – 'There are diversities of gifts,' wrote St Paul, 'but the same Spirit.' I had assumed goodness to be dull, and sureness the death of curiosity, but the sisters had converted their love into their lives, and they flourished with character and serenity. It was their quality to evoke affection, transfiguring those around them, and their virtues never changed nor showed themselves false.

Madonna especially grew more at ease, although her voice always mingled embarrassment with authority. Her secret vice, I discovered, was a passion for postage stamps.

'You will fly lower in heaven,' I told her, handing over a depressing row of British Fourpennies; but she was transformed, and the stamps, I learned, were not for herself but for her niece in Poland.

One morning a Polish Jew was baptized in the Christian faith. The Monsignor presided in the tiny chapel, and the young man knelt with a candle while two nuns sang hymns in 'cello voices. His parents, if they were strict Jews, might celebrate his funeral, for since he had abandoned their faith he would be dead to them. But he was happy and sure; he felt that he had not overthrown the faith of his fathers, but had built a new mansion in an old city. The Jewish convert to Christianity is different from others in this; he accepts Christ into the framework of his old belief not only as the Son of God but as the ultimate prophet of the Old Testament, the fruit of his nation's history.

It never occurred to the first Christians, all Jews, to abandon the synagogue, but they grouped themselves within it until the persecution of Agrippa I and the death of Stephen drove them abroad. Even then, the church in Jerusalem remained closed and rigid. St James, traditionally her first bishop, was long opposed to the conversion of Gentiles, and the breath of Christianity passed to Antioch and Caesarea where already men were discovering, in the mingled hope and ethic of the new religion, a refuge from the fitful gods of Rome.

Over the eastern Mediterranean the converts of St Paul were Greeks, or Jews half-Hellenized. They accepted Christ without the trappings of the Law, and when Jerusalem was crushed in AD 70 the break with the Judaic past was complete. It may be that Christ had himself known the Hellenic concept of love and the value it placed on individual man; if this was so, these elements, which followed the Greeks wherever they went, returned to them infused by a perception and a passion which they had never known.

The Hebraic and the Greek, in whose balance the whole of Western thought has rested for centuries, are still locked uneasily in Christendom – a rich but unhappy marriage between the masculine intellect and order of the West, and the feminine East, the Mediterranean, with its spirit of emotion and service. Clement and Origen had fought the same battle in Alexandria, as had Philo before, and the conflict had taken place as much in themselves as in the world about them. Even St Paul, whose mission was nearly mystic – the gospel of man's dwelling in Christ – was both Greek and Hebrew, whose message was tempered before the Jews to a voice of sympathy and wishfulness.

The importance of Israel waned in time and Hadrian permitted only Gentiles to return to his Aelia Capitolina. It is told that a Christian martyr gave the name of his city as the heavenly Jerusalem, but his judge tortured him, demanding to know in which country this city lay, for already the name was forgotten.

Constantine gave the city a golden age, the architectural beauty and material well-being of a pilgrim centre – and the dross of luxury too, 'a garrison, prostitutes, actors, buffoons, as in all other cities' (St Jerome). The exiled empress Eudocia and the emperor Justinian embellished her, and she became the fifth of the

Patriarchates of Byzantium. But power, the link of the religious with the secular, had wounded the older spirit, and the new churchmen were, in the tart words of Gibbon, 'more solicitous to explore the nature, than to practise the laws, of their founder'.

This hollowness, the sovereignty of theory over action, was a danger deep in Christianity. Judaism had controlled action so intricately that its meaning was easily forgotten; and Christ's argument was not with the body of the Law, from which he had grown as a child, but with small-mindedness, the deed without the spirit. The secret was not to impose duty but to evoke love. Yet now, in the early years of Byzantium, the significance of goodness was drowned by the prestige of theory, the dialectic of a still young church trying to understand its God and itself.

Jerusalem has little to show of all this, only an intimation of wall or sanctuary foundation, or the persistence of a name. But the mosaic floors on Olivet bear witness, in their modest way, to the ecclesiastical fervour, and Eudocia raised a shrine to St John Prodromos, the Baptist, which survived as the crypt of a medieval chapel. A bent passage leads from Christian Street to the upper church in a courtyard of lemon trees with a pretty, resonant well; its quietness is sudden, like the dying of a wind. A young priest led me round where the medieval sanctuary, built by Amalfitan merchants, had almost vanished under restorations. Now a classic cruciform basilica like the shrine which the Crusaders knew, it rested under a dented silver dome. An altar kept, inevitably, the fragments of the Baptist's skull, and among the ikons the dark, sepulchral face of John the Precursor had been painted by some fifteenth-century master when the art was still sublime.

Groping by fetid walls as if into a cellar, we descended to the shrine of Eudocia. I smelt dying flowers and saw broken wood stacked in a strand of sun. The priest turned a switch. There was a shimmering as if lanterns were trying to burn in the darkness, then the light went on and we stood in a church with the stark beauty of something grown naturally, like a cliff or tree, harmonious and true. So perfect was the skeleton that I looked for a trace of flesh, some fresco or mosaic, but there was none – the floor earth, the walls naked – only our shadows in the yellow bareness, and the trunk of a pillar lying disowned.

The priest's shoes crunched energetically back and forth in the shadow; it was as if we had been dropped into limbo, and even the colours of our clothes and faces were an outrage to its monotone. Medieval piles, rustic and crumbling, rose where columns had upheld a cupola, but around them the whorls of the trifoliate apse were magnificent in deep, unseeing windows, and in the almost fierce grandeur of their surfaces.

A further relic from these years lies north of the Damascus Gate – a mosaic floor from the Armenian church to St Polyeucht, a soldier-martyr of the third century. Perhaps the first monument to the Unknown Warrior, it is inscribed 'to the memory and salvation of the souls of all Armenians whose names are known by God alone', and lies above a grave filled with the jumbled bones of soldiers.

The old caretaker emerged as I stood there.

'Birds,' he said.

'Birds?'

He began wiping the huge floor with a damp cloth, and out of the greyed mosaic the colours came delicate and luminous, as if a dusk landscape were suddenly relit by sun. From an urn a supple vine sprang – a classical gesture – and held forty birds gracefully confined, each in a tress of its stem. Domestic and well-fed, pecking at the grapes which dangled round them, they seemed to have entered a mosaic paradise. The horny legs and dark, muted tails of the peacocks, the lissome necks of herons, were the fruit of long observation, and the old man easily pointed out their many kinds, until bemused by the flamingo. I stared entranced – how intimate and ordered they were! – and felt obscurely glad that in the midst of their wrangles over the Double Nature and the *Theotokos*, Nestorianism and Monophysitism, men had noticed so minutely the innocence about them, and had lifted it with love and cunning out of time.

The Monastery of the Cross in the New City is also of these years, built by King Tatian of Georgia on the place where legend set the tree which had formed the gibbet of Christ. Countlessly restored, it appears Byzantine still, high and windowless and spattered with half-visible terraces, more fortress than sanctuary. The ante-chapel is part Crusader, with the crevice enshrined where the holy tree had stood; and the church is rich with frescoed piers, grown from pale floors as sombre-wooded trees from the light earth, and ikons shine in landscapes of red-gold. I passed through doors heavy in iron, and round the high nave on Tatian's faint mosaics. From their pillars the eleventh-century saints scrutinized me disapprovingly, waving their books and crosses in little simian hands, or stood back in stillness, long and baleful, with sad-faced angels whose wings made light and painless their slender feet on earth.

Yet more heady and enduring than anything which Byzantium has left in stone is the Orthodox Church itself, whose Patriarch in Jerusalem claims direct succession from Marcus, the city's bishop in the time of Hadrian. Ritual and tradition armour it – 'the everlasting boundaries which our fathers have set' (St John Damascene, *On Icons* ii.12) – and its Holy Liturgy is a glinting, talismanic archaism, filled with the casual beauty of litany and intimate processions, incense-drunken priests and the magic of symbol. The empire is gone which echoed once the monarchy of Christ in heaven, but the church is still the palace of Divinity on earth, in whom the New Jerusalem is already incarnate. Its bishops rule in place of God, and the splendour of the Liturgy mirrors the hosannas in paradise. When the Patriarch stands in the Catholicon of the Holy Sepulchre, the Church Invisible is praying with him, the saints and angels whose images glisten in a hierarchic family on every iconostasis, and grant the worshipper a glimpse of heaven.

'When the priest administers the sacrament he is transformed,' a Russian nun told me. 'He is no longer himself. Even if he is drunk at the altar, angels hold the chalice in his hands.' She was a tiny figure, delicately old, walking with a crutch in the garden of a convent in Bethany.

'The transfiguration of the human soul, who can penetrate it? The gap between man and his Creator is not so great with us as with the Roman Catholics. We believe that God gave us freedom naturally out of perfect love, even when in Adam we were innocent of knowledge. We are not tainted with primal guilt. We say only that man inherited the corruption of Adam, that his soul is distorted, not utterly changed; that he may still find God within him, as it was said of St Pachomius, that "in the mirror of his heart's innocence he knew the unseen God".'

She spoke with modulation, as if from much reading and articulated thought, moving a blue-veined hand to form her phrases in the air.

'Perhaps the Eastern church looks on things with more emotion than the West,' she said. 'We are intuitive, the Latins more legalistic. But can one say who is right? It is as if many people were looking at this book.' She sat at a garden table where a Russian hymnal lay. 'Some see the top, some the spine, some only an edge. Yet the object remains. We see truly, but not completely.'

'And what of those who find the book meaningless,' I asked, 'those who view its creation as a chance of nature?'

'Some,' she said quietly, 'would claim that only the intellect may understand. But truth is a two-edged sword. Divine grace does not operate through the mind, or else only the clever would reach God. What matters is the heart. St Augustine – a Latin saint – said that belief brings understanding, not the other way around. *Credo ut intelligam*.'

'There are some,' I said, thinking of certain Orthodox priests, 'who believe without appearing to understand; who seem to live in vegetable faith.'

She was silent a moment, her face surrounded ethereally in the white wimple-veil where her high forehead tapered to a wisp of pixie hair.

'Who is perfect? Are you? Am I?' It was the gentlest rebuke. 'Faith, you see, is like the sun on a mountain. Many men walk there. The scientist may understand the ultra-violet rays. An ordinary person simply feels the heat; and even a blind man may be warm. It can satisfy all our faculties. God gave us spirit, mind and body. Each has its sphere of action. If one is left barren, the harmony is gone. There are some, I know, whose brains are idle; but there are others whose hearts remain cold. Which of these states is sadder?'

Her eyes laughed at me, suddenly fey.

'In Russia,' she continued, 'we used to have people called "Fools for Christ"; they gave up the mind in favour of intuition. I remember them as a child in St Petersburg. They had gifts of prophecy and saw visions.'

It was the heart which mattered, she said again. 'Love which flows naturally, giving freedom to others, as God gave freedom to us. Only the love which demands is dangerous and shows trouble in the soul, the need for receiving instead of giving.'

She rose to walk again, murmuring in afterthought: 'Of course I do not speak about the love between a man and a woman. That is more complicated.'

We went among trees where the convent schoolchildren were playing. She walked with pain, but buoyantly. She was grateful to God, she said, that suffering had given her spiritual perception. 'Beyond every physical sign and inside every material process, mystical events go on . . .'

I wondered what lay between us. I listened to her entranced but untouched, like those biblical people who have ears but hear not. The bright sky had darkened in the garden. We heard the singing of unseen birds in a selfish extravagance of joy. She talked as if from some jewelled casket, which enclosed her naturally and answered exactly to the shape of her being. We came out to the courtyard under trees, where the desert heaved luminous and cruel, and I felt astonished that this breeding-place of intoxicated prophets had formed, in a sense, her silver radiance; that so much in a single person might be universal, the desert loneliness in the world, yearnings and dreams and the temples built around them.

The Greek Orthodox Patriarchate is in the city's Christian quarter and leans on the Church of the Holy Sepulchre in jumbled heaps of domes and stairs. Bishops and archimandrites keep olympian state, portentous with politics and ceremonial like Dark Age popes. The complex of convents is filled with chapels, courts and gardens where refugee children come at noon for meals, their feet light on the passageways.

But the deep, low churches of Constantine are gone. The timber roofs, the long chancels where all the celebrants could kneel together, the delicate wooden frames of clerestory windows, all vanished with the hillside forests, giving place to the high dome of Byzantium. And with the hardening of the Liturgy as early as Justinian's reign the iconostasis replaced the little stone balustrades whose sockets may be seen in the rock of church excavations, where all else is lost.

Yet the many-marbled floors, the choice, sugar-like capitals and numinous mosaic glitter remained. In smaller churches the figures of saints were frescoed in staring, Syrian postures without the mystery of Constantinople or the grace of Rome, but although these were ruined centuries ago, new shrines stand on their foundations and have sometimes preserved their names. Thrust in the bulk of other walls, their exterior shapes are lost – Byzantine even in this, that the classical love of outer beauty now looks inward. There remain only shreds from the old lustre, and the pleasure of peaceful courts. Inside is an air of musty benignity, a torrent of lamps from arris vaulting, an eighteenth-century gilded iconostasis, the caress of a cobweb or two and a threadbare *epitaphios*. All is tarnished and familiar: the common-room for some college of easy-going saints.

Only here and there a strangeness makes itself remembered: the Church of St Dimitri, fragrant in the lemon gardens of the Orthodox Patriarchate; St Mary the Virgin whose Greek nuns sit spinning, and stare with the pinched faces of Peloponnesian crones; and the roofless chancel of St Thomas, where cassia trees grow wild, and where 'Moslems and Jews may not enter, for by decree of Heaven they would die. The door therefore is shut lest such should go there, not knowing this' (Jean Doublan, *Le Voyage de la Terre Sainte*, Paris, 1657). But most pleasing is St Euthymius – a tiny chapel where the queens of Trebizond worshipped, and a dazzling garden, white with jasmine and doves.

Most of these churches lie close to the Patriarchate, and the Christian quarter round them is crossed with steep, clean alleys. An air of prosperity is about. Christians occupy more than a third of the Old City although they number only eleven thousand, a fifth of the Moslem population.

St Francis Street, the spine of the Latin community, grows quiet in its western stretches, sending alleys south by the Roman Catholic hospice of Casa Nova, and the Latin Patriarchate, a nightmare of the neo-Gothic. To its north is the jungle of the Terra Sancta, where the Franciscans have lived for more than four hundred years, extending their ownership over properties all around, and once the only haven of pilgrims. Now its vaulted avenues run through august courtyards and its Church of St Saviour is a blast of *fare figura*, a too-rich corner of Trastevere.

South of David Street the ways are still narrower, the houses so massed that they swallow churches easily. The Syrian Orthodox – schismatic since the fifth century for their views on the nature of Christ – number scarcely more than a hundred people in the city, but their Church of St Mark is old with a Crusader gateway. Its people form an unchanging, country sect. They believe that the Last Supper took place in their church and that St Peter found refuge there after the angels had freed him from prison. They keep a portrait of the Virgin 'painted by St Luke'; the service is still read in Syriac, the language of Christ, and the Patriarchs are buried under the floors in the old manner, robed and embalmed on episcopal thrones.

Yet the quarter around them belongs to the Armenians, whose kingdom was the pawn of empires in antiquity and the first, it is said, to become Christian. They have been in Jerusalem since the fourth century or earlier, and most of the sector was bought from the Georgians, whose wealth declined with the fortunes of their country, until they vanished from the city a hundred years ago. The Armenian compound is spacious and dignified, a community self-contained in its walls, with an arcaded seminary and a cruciform hall, a library and the 'House of Annas'. The silence is one with the people, who seem to live pleasantly in the worn spaces, as if in some university of the spirit.

In the west a garden of bleached pine trees runs to the city ramparts within, embrasures stifled by the high-grown earth. Manuscripts in the library-church of St Theodorus are ranged in cupboards round the nave – Gospels and the works of church fathers, which give a history of Armenian illumination over nine centuries far back to the child-like figures and bright, elementary colours of northern Syria. An old bishop opened the books delicately, and I peered into the mind of another race: intent, ascetic people and a sleek, cursive script; men who worked with hairs for brushes secretly, year after year, on a few chapters of teaching, because these were the words of God. Most beautiful is the art of Thoros Roslin, whose tints remain exquisite after seven hundred years – ground lapis lazuli for depths of blue, and purples and reds from an obscure Armenian worm whose dye had clothed the last Byzantine kings. The compositions of the Yerzinka Bible are a school of illumination in themselves, and the austerity never eases, but even in the nineteenth century draws its pining, elegiac figures as if the world's view of God had never changed.

The Church of St James, which is the core of the Armenian convent, sprang up in medieval times and devoured a Georgian monastery and Byzantine chapel, but its courtyard and façade have lost their old proportions. Wood and iron semantra hung outside, and moaned dreamily when I tapped them. I opened the iron door and walked down the piers of a nave superbly built, where painted saints communed with one another across the dark – a cruciform church whose pillars held a complex dome of star-shaped ribs, like the Moorish cupolas of Spain. Across its floors moved stalks of harvest light, throwing haloes over remote martyrs and prophets; and beyond a shallow step – a classic Armenian feature – the communion table rose tall and tapering, like a Siamese altar. From this great nave the aisles were brushed aside. Kutayha tiles vanished under the canvases of stained, sentimental portraiture, and even these were garlanded in lamps and baubles.

The church is full of secrets. In the northern aisle I found the gilded 'Throne of St James', and bijou chapels whose doors were of tortoiseshell set with mother-of-pearl, and silver fish-shaped handles. Below an altar, enshrined in trembling lantern flames, 'the head of the apostle St James lies buried'; and a priest told me that the body of James the brother of Christ rested under the high altar, and that the last Armenian queen and princes of Cilicia were interred about the walls.

Hidden doors swung open from the panelling and led steeply between hollow walls to little, garnished chapels, and behind a curtain a low door guarded the treasury in the ancient shrine of St Menas – pieces less rich but more beautiful than those of the Greeks: the work of Armenian craftsmen in Istanbul, Persia and Van. Gold- and silver-threaded vestments, whose woven designs were smooth and fine as paintings; banners and chalices, set with Indian stones, mitres and chasubles, a cope cut from the silk tent which Napoleon made at Jaffa; a crosier twined of golden snakes, crowned with a diamond cross; the sceptre of King Hattun II, formed from a single piece of amber and inherited by the last Armenian king – all these lay unseen in the chapel.

I entered the sacristy in the north, still Georgian in part, and crossed to the chapel of Echtiamadzin, which was once an arcade, its important door absurd now, and nastily painted. In the chapel a few candles burnt. A woman lay in a coffin, a sheaf of flowers on her breast: an elderly peasant with a greyed face, dressed in her everyday clothes. Momentarily I thought she was a statue, until I saw the faint web of wrinkles and the quarter-smile made bare by tightening skin. The birds were singing outside, and from a window a spray of light crept towards her over the floor.

In a case were rocks from Sinai, kept for pilgrims to touch who cannot travel there. I looked about the chapel with its naïve tiles, but the architecture had died. Only the little woman appeared alive, clasping her garish flowers, death new and light on her.

I went out of the Damascus Gate along the Nablus road – a thread of Christianity through the new town. Country women sat begging in the shadows, their babies sleeping across their knees. Under a charred scarp was the 'Grotto of Jeremiah', where legend says that he composed his lamentations; but a notice over the entrance read 'Store for Pananis', and it turned out to be a depot for bananas – a pleasant end for the lair of so dismal a prophet.

The Garden Tomb was nearby, cut in the emaciated knoll which General Gordon thought to be Calvary. He imagined Jerusalem as a skeleton lying on its side, with its feet in the Pool of Siloam and its head on this hillock; and others, adding spice to the fiction, decided that the place resembled a skull pocked by two cisterns like eye-sockets, and that it must be Golgotha. Already a tomb had been discovered beneath it, and a falsified inscription led to an archaeological and religious frenzy which only slowly died. Now no church or archaeologist supports its claim to holiness, but an English society runs it with impassioned efficiency and sells pamphlets at the gate.

It is a place in which one would like to believe – a small, triple sepulchre, pale-stoned and left in its simplicity. Sitting among its trees, I heard an onrush of tourist-guides propounding its inviolable claims, pointing out medieval troughs and conduits as the apse of a ruined chapel – 'built by early Christians to enclose the holy sepulchre' – and there was a dutiful clicking of cameras.

Tombs of many ages fill the ridges. Saladin's warriors were

buried in their armour all around, and sometimes Roman sarcophagi are found, and Byzantine jewellery. The Garden Tomb, it seems, is part of a Herodian necropolis which the Dominicans discovered while they were searching for the Basilica of St Stephen. This, built on the supposed place of his stoning, they also found, and raised a new sanctuary on its mosaic floors where Eudocia, its foundress, had been buried a millennium and a half before.

The Dominicans have their convent and a famous biblical school here, and the strong, ordered cloisters suit them, as the Dormition's hallowed seclusion suits the Benedictines, and the devout chaos of the Terra Sancta the Franciscans. The Dominicans are scholars, whose erudition may be mingled with drollery or earnestness, a penchant for Hinduism or a love of Rousseau. Père de Vaux, the ex-director, is a specialist in the Old Testament and the Dead Sea Scrolls: a kind, roguish-looking monk; while the present director, Père Benoit, is a New Testament scholar with a passion for yoga. The place is like some eccentric and animated campus of heaven; but the well-formed corridors, the vast, severed columns under pines, the austere church, all echo a weight and elegance of learning, and under the courtyard colonnades I lifted iron slabs from Byzantine tombs, in whose inscriptions and rested bones was the continuity of faith which I had sensed: 'He who puts his trust in the Most High', 'the Lord is my Light'.

Along the bared rim of No-Man's-Land the walls have flopped into dust, and the Mandelbaum Gate has gone. St. George's cathedral close is gay with flowering trees, a school and a cloistered hospice on which the orient has been laid carefully with hung carpets and tiles. Here the Anglican Archbishop in Jerusalem lives, whose see extends from Libya to Iran; and the hospice is quiet with the trudge of trusted servants.

Beyond is the American Colony, where in 1881 a charitable community was settled by a Chicago lawyer whose descendants still run the Spafford Children's Hospital in the Old City, and keep a gracious hospice. The way descends to a glade of thinning trees, and squares of light appear at evening where hotels crawl along the tail of Mount Scopus by the friendly gardens of the British School of Archaeology.

A wind rose as the sun drowned in the hills. I saw a muezzin leaning from the minaret of the mosque of Sheikh Jarrah – the last in Jerusalem to spurn a microphone – and his call came on the Judean air in a *legato* of pure sadness.

'La -llah illa -llah . . .' – the old, resplendent truth that God is One; and the Eastern City poured its answers into the twilit sky, thirteen hundred years of strange, insistent voices, it seemed, gathered into an evening. On the edge of the dark the Crusaders of de Bouillon lumbered upward from the shallow, walnut valley, with their pennants and long shields, singing and weeping to the holy city. Then the Moslem sea closed over them, and Jerusalem became again only a dream in the Western consciousness, a dream more beautiful unrealized. Out of the wastes of Judea rose the soft hills of Giorgione's imagined land, the weird, striated bluffs of Filippo Lippi, the mild, watered valleys of the later Florentines.

And what is left now of the Jerusalem of Christ? A scattering of stones, a ruffled slab, a chance capital. Scarcely a site is proof against enquiry. But the anger remains, divided against itself, casting out prophets. The tints of the past are deep and savage, reaching out of antiquity, breaking and recreating, dislodging and assembling old defences and ideas. The very stones seem shaped by suffering, and the people in every century have known that they lived in an inheritance wider than its walls, have seen the New Jerusalem as a baptism of the old at the end of time.

'I saw a new heaven and a new earth:' runs the Revelation of St John the Divine, 'for the first heaven and the first earth were passed away; and there was no more sea. And I John saw the holy city, new Jerusalem, coming down from God out of heaven, prepared as a bride adorned for her husband. And I heard a great voice out of heaven saying, Behold, the tabernacle of God is with man . . . And God shall wipe away all tears from their eyes; and there shall be no more death, neither sorrow, nor crying, neither shall there be any more pain: for the former things are passed away.'

Immortal dream.

10

The Dome of the Rock

A good work is as a good tree; its root firmly fixed
and its branches in the heaven.
(Koran 14)

In the deserts of Arabia a Bedou may ride for weeks on an undulant yellow sea which the wind has eased to nothing greater than ripples, and the few things which he finds in his solitude – a rock, an acacia bush – attain a disquieting significance. The blistered bark, the sculptural flow of stone, are vibrant in their sunlit wilderness, and a feeling of wonder comes over him, or a numinous fear, so that tribesmen sense God in the trees and rocks; and sometimes, even in the Old Testament, the word rock is used in place of God; 'He is the Rock' (Deuteronomy 32:4), 'the Rock that begat thee' (Deuteronomy 32:18).

The meteorite in the Kaaba at Mecca is the greatest of these idols, older than the faith of Mahomet and a memory from times when Arabia knew only astral deities, sybil-queens and stone-worship. But caravans, bringing their produce north and south, carried the rumour of a single God along the eternal ways to merchant cities. Half-assimilated Jewish tribes settled along the coasts, and Monophysite Christians came. Mahomet knew these peoples and debated with them, and his revelations are filled with Jewish law and fragmented history. His followers first turned toward Jerusalem to pray, and for a moment she was the holiest of their cities, the centre of the world. But the Prophet grew disenchanted with the Jews, believing not that their religion was false but that they had strayed from its purity. He saw himself as the last seer of the Old Testament, the spiritual heir of Abraham, Moses and Solomon, and when at last he turned from Jerusalem to Mecca, it was a rejection of the Jews themselves, not of the structure of their belief, for 'Who but a madman would reject the religion of Abraham? We have chosen him in this world and in the next he will be among the just' (Koran 2:124).

In the middle of the seventh century the progress of the exiled Prophet in the Hejaz went unheard among the conflicts of Persia and Byzantium. Arabia was a half-known country, a drift of tribesmen in the north, and beyond them the same secluded cities as had brought perfumes and incense to Rome – Arabia Odorifera, far away and legendary in richness. But the press of population in constricted pastures, the magic of the One God and the genius of His Prophet carried the Arabs to Egypt and Syria soon after his death in AD 632, and seventy years later they had broken into Spain and were marching on the borders of China.

Jerusalem fell in 638 and was granted clemency by the caliph Omar who met her Patriarch Sophronius on the Mount of Olives to discuss peace. 'Verily, you are assured of the complete security of your lives, your goods, and your churches, which will not be inhabited nor destroyed by the Moslems . . .' So the aged Damascene Patriarch took the little negroid caliph into the holy city and as they approached, runs a tale, it became the servant's turn to ride Omar's camel, and he dismounted and entered in rags, austere and democratic in the earliest tradition of Islam.

He asked to be conducted to the site of the Temple of Solomon, and Sophronius, fearing that he meant to rebuild it, took him instead to the Church of the Holy Sepulchre. As the caliph's hour for devotions drew near the Patriarch suggested that he pray there, but he refused: 'If I had prayed inside the church thou wouldst have lost it; the believers would have taken it from thee, saying, "Omar prayed here."' So he knelt near its entrance where, as he had foretold, a mosque arose to his memory, and the Omariyah in the west is still a monument to his mildness and wisdom.

Sophronius took him to other churches but Omar, entering a doorway cluttered with filth, came on his knees through the sewer to the Temple area, and saw the great rock at its centre – the place of his people's adopted prophets. Christians, angry with the Jews for inciting the Persian invasion of 614, had used the Temple mount for refuse, defiling the sacred rock, the *lapis pertusus*, which the Jews had anointed with tears and oil since the time of Constantine. With his own hands the caliph lifted the dung from the summit and hurled it into the Kidron valley, and a wooden mosque was built alone on the terraces.

All this may be legend, yet underneath, like ruins gilded over by the earth, the truths are there in harder shapes, and certainly Omar permitted the Jews, exiled by Heraclius, to return to the city; and from their earliest days the Moslems honoured the rock. Its legends were treasured and spun again; upon its altar Abraham had prepared to offer Isaac to God, and Jacob had fallen asleep and seen the angels climbing between its crest and heaven. Only the black boulder of the Kaaba is more sacred, because it fell as a gift from the skies, but at the resurrection it will come to the rock of Jerusalem with greetings, for this is the Stone of Paradise and foundation of the world, beneath whose mountain is the gate to the Celestial City.

Moslems say that Mahomet flew from Mecca on his mare, el-Burak, and alighted upon the hill's summit. The Koran declares 'Glory be to Him who carried His servant by night from the Sacred Mosque to the Faraway Mosque' (Koran 17:1), and although in mystic interpretation the 'Faraway Mosque' is God Himself, popular imagination conceived it to be the Temple of Jerusalem, the most distant point of Moslem pilgrimage. From it the angel Gabriel lifted Mahomet into the stars, where he saw a Dantesque heaven filled with allegory, sinners in 'the wind-blown ashes of their deeds' and the gardens of eternity where the blessed lay, their good deeds blossomed into trees and flowers.

So the Moslems dealt kindly with Jerusalem, accepting her largely Semitic population as half-brothers. The taxes which had fattened the court at Byzantium were diverted to the coffers of the Caliphate, and the Christians and Jews effaced themselves before an Arab aristocracy which fulfilled the Bedouin ideal of warrior overlords. In time the sanctity of the city deepened. Lying within the confines of those countries which the orthodox caliphs conquered, she became part of Moslem holy land, the personal patrimony of Allah to His faithful. The city was named *El-Kuds*, 'the Holy', and *Thalith el Haramain*, the third of the sacred cities after Mecca and Medinah; and some even said that the temple of *as-Sakhra*, 'the Rock', was the first among shrines.

'I have asked the prophet which is the most radiant city in the world,' averred a Companion of Mahomet, 'and he answered "Jerusalem"'; and the hero Ali claimed that she lay nearer to heaven than anywhere else in the world, a fragment from paradise. The friends and soldiers of Mahomet were entombed round the walls where Adam and Abraham were believed to have been buried. Here Jesus had spoken in his cradle and Mary had lived 'a virgin unknown to mortal man' (Koran 19:20). Whoever died there would be assured of salvation, and when the angel Israfil blew the trumpet of resurrection from the rock, *Yom-el-gyama* – the Day of Judgment – would be proclaimed from the Mount of Olives by Jesus Christ, the second among prophets.

For a generation, only the frail wooden mosque of Omar stood on the Temple esplanade and the Arabs seemed unwilling to emulate the buildings of the people whom they had conquered. But in 687 'Abd-el-Malik, the caliph in Damascus, decided to set up in his dominions a centre of pilgrimage which would rival Mecca, then in the hands of enemies. No more would the faithful journey to the Hejaz, he declared, but to Jerusalem; 'this Rock, of which it is reported that upon it the Apostle of God set his foot when he ascended into heaven, shall be unto you in the place of the Kaaba' (Yaqubi, *History* II). Perhaps, too, the faithful had been enticed by the Church of the Holy Sepulchre, splendid even after Persian fires, and the caliph 'was moved lest it should dazzle the minds of the Muslims, and hence erected above the Rock the dome which is now to be seen there' (Muqaddasi).

These motives, more shrewd than pious, were typical of the Damascus rulers, but the shrine which the caliph raised – the first great building of Islam – is perfect as a fruit or flower, resplendent without vanity, and all its richness garnered into clear, harmonious forms. The long architectural struggle to place a dome beautifully on an angular base here reached its fruition – the octagon of lowspread walls blowing a golden bubble into the sky, delicate and restful, a crown and a balm.

No Arabian architects could have raised such a building, and the names which have survived – ibn Haywa and ibn Sallam – are those only of administrators. The arts of the Damascus caliphs – poetry and song – were still those of the desert, impassioned, virile and pagan. The court was a mixture of splendour and informality, licentiousness undisguised in a silken piety, and only a few years after Omar had entered Jerusalem with no other luxury than a sack of dates, the Commanders of the Faithful were tippling with forbidden wine and building pleasure-palaces in the desert. But to administer or beautify their cities they had to turn to those whom they had overcome, and the art of early Islam grew up in the arms of Byzantium, its craftsmen Hellenized Syrians.

So the Dome of the Rock was no creature of nomad genius but a child of the Mediterranean, of the Rotunda in the Church of the Holy Sepulchre, whose measurements it followed and whose ancestry reaches far back to Santa Costanza and a family of old Roman giants – the mausolea of emperors, the Pantheon and the Minerva Medica. The Church of the Ascension in Jerusalem was already built, with the upper church of the Virgin's Tomb, the Octagon at Bethlehem and others scattered over northern Syria, perhaps the birthplace of the octagon in architecture.

Yet walking through the wraith of Herod's Temple after dawn – the paved loneliness of a mountain plateau – I saw the sanctuary rising in a pure Islamic ripeness from the earth. Mahomet's ban on images had swept away the whole train of painted warrior-prophets which would otherwise have crept about its walls, and outside, the mosaics of flowers and leaves which covered the upper base and drum had been replaced in the time of Suleiman by faience tiles from Persia, since renewed.

Over the pavements the cypress trees moaned together in dark choirs, and blind, fragile men haunted the esplanade, the tap of their sticks insistent on walls, as if Islam were dying in the courts of its splendour. Pines too, vast and drunk under the sun, had outlived their strength, and flowers dropped their petals reluctantly like tears in shaded gardens. I came to the sanctuary platform, starred by the ascent of many steps. Above each stairway ran tall arcades – a dance of three medieval arches where the scales of Judgment Day will hang – and I felt their shadows move over me as I went.

The shrine stood in the diamond of the morning. Small porches were at its compass-points on cloudy columns; windows delicate with faience lattices; the tiles in their ecstasy of blue – cornflower, cobalt and lapis lazuli. These were the Persian patterns of Kashan renewed, lustrous and half-barbaric. I saw two panels of dappled marble which seemed to depict a pair of birds drinking from a vase

– swallows, say Moslems, which abused King Solomon, who turned them into stone.

At the entrance of the sanctuary an old man took my shoes and gave me slippers. I went from blinding sun into shadow; the doors closed behind. In its twilight the shrine lay open like a casket: the richness of a young empire, vibrant and sure, poured into the harmony which older worlds had set. It was gentle and iridescent, scarcely tangible. From the flaring surfaces I had stepped into a building's heart, pervaded by visions and ideas. Softly the ambulatory pushed its columns through the gloom, went flowing on before me as I walked.

The outer walls were veined in marble rivers, disturbed and delicate, silken to touch. Even the tie-beams of arcades were gilded fastidiously underneath in vines like scrolls and trumpets. The stained-glass windows, many of them old, appeared to shed no light, but like illumined pages hung translucent in the darkness. The sun crept in at will, dreamt here and there in bubbles or stood in the muted chambers of the doors. A worshipper could sleepwalk in its night forever.

At its centre above the rock the marble columns reached to a dazzled cylinder, whose mosaics were awakening to the sun beneath the dome, the fourteenth-century work of Indian craftsmen. The pious walked in silence clockwise, and touched their foreheads to the ground in prayer, going through their actions carefully – standing, bending, the hands clasped on the stomach or patting the knees: a formal and dignified service which has remained unchanged for centuries. There was nothing self-conscious in the gestures, for the Moslem's humility is natural. No sublime Pantocrator is spread across his dome, no god uplifts the eye. Man is not deified in the Orthodox way, nor is the church the echo of paradise. The Dome of the Rock has become deeply Islamic, enclosing its people with an earthbound radiance – intimate and undemanding. No anguish, no guilt, no ecstasy. God, the Immeasurable, makes little call upon the intellect. His mosque is dark and clouds the eye, a hall for the obedience of servants' prayers.

God is approached reverently as a king, not intimately as a friend. His people are dust in the palm of the universe. 'God leads astray' the Koran says often and terribly – an old Semitic concept. He chooses only whom He will, and 'there are those whose heart he wishes not to purify' (Koran 5:46). This sadness runs in a grey strand through Islamic thought. Sin is no fall from spiritual grace, no blow to the loving Saviour, but merely a breaking of law, and repentance does not find the personal absolution of a Christ. No inner guilt is salved, no rush of regeneration comes, for these are the fruit of unknown bonds with God.

But the pith of Islam is justice and charity. Sublime for its age and people, the dangers embodied there are no more its essense than empty action is the spirit of Judaism, or self-absorption a Christian cult. And the Moslem God is, in a sense, more pure than the God of Christ or Moses. He sent no son and chose no special people. His laws were as simple and democratic as theirs. The sadness of ideals is only that man falls short of them. The first inspiration dies. The truth is forgotten which raised the golden Dome. The empire itself splintered which, with seven years' revenue from Egypt, brought into existence this god-sent harmony.

Into the building's beauty the rock heaves like a wave – primeval nature pressed up as if by earthquake through the elaborate floors. Its troughs and holes are indecipherable, except where the architect trimmed it for symmetry, and the Crusaders notched an altar. The dome lights it in a circlet of mosaics, the gift of Byzantium, muted and celestial, covering the whole drum and inner arches; but already their mixed motifs are from the world of Damascus caliphs. Out of bulbous urns the Hellenistic vines come dark to their gold sky. Greek craftsmen, denied the portrayal of man or beast, created them eerie and predatory. They curl their fronds above like oriental dancers, waltzing in green and gold, and mother-of-pearl glints in dew-drops on their urns – urns grown ebullient in the half-light, crowned with Sassanian wings; urns for the smoke of *djinns* and consummation of arcane desires.

'This Qubbat was built by the servant of God', runs an inscription on the inner arcade, ''Abdullah al-Imam, the Prince of the Believers, al-Ma'moon, in the year 72 AH [AD 691], may God accept this and be pleased with him. Amen.' So the Abbasid caliph al-Ma'moon, hoping to partake of the building's glory, erased the name of 'Abd-el-Malik from the inscription, but never changed the date.

The Crusaders came, turned the building into the 'Templum

Domini' and fastened a gold and diamond Saviour to its door. They covered the rock in marble to protect it from the chippings of the pious, and ringed it with a handsome iron screen, still kept in the museum. But for less than ninety years did the cross shine on the Dome, though the Templars, when they returned to Europe, began to build their churches – London's Temple, Aix la Chapelle, Metz, Laon – in its image.

Over the earlier Islamic centuries the repairs were meticulous and tasteful, and the sultans recorded them in the Kufic script which is itself an art: Saladin, who 'ordered the renovation of the gilding of this Holy Dome'; Sultan Mahomet, 'God's shadow on earth and executor of His commands'; Suleiman the Magnificent, 'Father of Conquests'; and Khan-May, 'Sultan of the Two Continents and the Two Seas'.

In a reliquary a few hairs from Mahomet's beard are kept; and, placing my hand through a hole, I touched the stone which was marked by his foot as he mounted to heaven. Two Moorish women fondled its grille. I stood near a jasper slab which covers the legendary grave of Solomon, and sketched the mosaic plants. A sheikh came up to me, afraid that I was a Jew annotating the sanctuary's riches for some evil, but was reassured by the gaucherie of my drawings.

'Did you know,' he asked, 'that in this rock is a cave where all prayers are answered?'

We descended to a soft-lit chamber, its walls unfissured, but here and there washed dark.

'Listen to the voices,' he said.

I listened to the stone for its voice; but I only heard American tourists.

'No. Other voices. They come from below, from the *Bir el-Arwah*, the Well of Spirits. Don't you hear them?'

We stood silent in the soul of the rock. Sounds came in shadows, passing away before I knew them. He stamped his foot, and a creature seemed to moan under the marble flagstones.

'The great ones have known God here,' he said. 'Mahomet – may God be merciful to him! – Solomon, Elijah. Beneath us is the Well of Souls. Sometimes the voices of the dead can be heard, like waters, praying together. A wall was built over it because our women would set their mouths at the cracks and gossip to the spirits.'

Peasant women with a picnic of bread and tomatoes prostrated themselves on the floor, and ascended the stairs again. The old man went away, and I walked alone round the rock walls, as if there was more to discover. The Jews and Moslems say that this is the world's foundation-stone, which David uncovered, lying above the abyss of Chaos and all the waters of the world. As Mahomet journeyed to heaven it rose to follow him, but was held lightly back by Gabriel, whose fingermarks are dimpled in it still. Some believe that here the rivers of paradise spring up, clouds live and the cool winds pray to God before they blow; seventy thousand angels guard the cave forever, and prophets come invisibly to pray.

I stamped my foot on the marble as the old man had done, but heard nothing. Above me a smooth hole had been bored in antiquity from the rock surface to the cave – the 'perforated stone' which the Jews still hallowed early in the fourth century. Its purpose is unknown, but its past may be steeped in awesome holiness: the altar of Herod's Temple, the blood of sacrifice dripping to the cavern where I stood; even the altar of Solomon, where the Jebusite threshed at the wheat in the days of his freedom.

It was full morning when I walked over the sloping roofs of the Dome of the Rock. Arab historians tell that the architects refused the extra gold which the caliph offered them, and asked that it be melted down instead and spread over the cupola. But this vanished years ago, and the dome itself fell early in the eleventh century, and was last restored in bronze aluminium.

I climbed a ladder up the drum, opened a flap in the dome and crept between the golden outer cupola and the wooden inner one. The whole frame whined and snored as the sun expanded it. Through the quaint pillars of a dust-covered gallery, cheerfully and rather carelessly painted, I looked down to the rock through glittering whorls of light, as through the spheres of Dante's paradise.

From the flap in the dome I could see the whole *Haram es-Sherif*, the Noble Sanctuary, below – a stone-flagged field, one-fifth of the walled city, where even the Dome of the Rock seems lost. High over the Kidron and Gehenna east and south, it was lifted in the shield of the ramparts, and the Mount of Olives peered over the eastern walls. The deep bell-notes of the Holy Sepulchre crossed the Tyropoeon valley, and the dome re-echoed them cynically.

The minarets are on three sides, two restored but two high and complete. Mameluke-built and strong, their tips are crowned with balconies on honeycomb corbelling, and the Ghawanmeh in the north-west is dressed in columels whose capitals show wasted figures of Christ, plucked from the vanished Chapel of Repose. To the north the *Haram* walls are pierced by deep, handsome gates with glorious names – Gate of the Tribes, Gate of Darkness and the Gate Ghawanmeh – and on the west the graves of Moslem heroes are immured in flaking rooms. Other gates lead into the turmoil of the city: the entrance of the Moors above the Wailing Wall; the Bab Qattanin of the sultan Tingiz, who liked fierce, stalactic gates and tooth-like lintels; the Gate of the Chain, the Beautiful Gate of medieval times, larger than any, with domes and Crusader columns.

I glimpsed a fountain of Suleiman the Magnificent in the street beyond, set with the tracery of a Crusader rose-window, the centuries fused and mellow. Children were clambering in and out of the dry pool, and demanded *backsheesh* in a slatternly fashion. I glanced at the pavement in the great entrance and saw ridged Roman slabs which must have lain there since the time of Herod. In his reign the road had come down wide and straight from the Citadel to the Temple, passing across Wilson's buried arch and over these time-smoothed pavements through the gate. Christ must have passed over them as he taught in his last years.

Many smaller buildings are sprinkled over the *Haram es-Sherif*. I saw the Cupolette of the Ascension, draped in columns, elegant and ignored; the turgid dome of the Qaitbey fountain; a fourteenth-century marble summer pulpit, confected of many ages; and a *mihrab* dedicated, in the eclectic Moslem way, to the Virgin Mary.

There was a legion of cisterns and fountains too, and a low mosque called the Throne of Solomon glued to the eastern walls. Solomon had grown old there and fearing that the *djinns* would destroy his works, propped himself upon his throne in death. Many days passed, and people thought that the king slept. But at last a worm came and gnawed the wood of the staff on which he leant, so that his body tumbled down and the demons despoiled his kingdom.

The Dome of the Small Rock was a gracious Crusader chapel once, enshrining a piece of the hill which in legend Nebuchadnezzar cut from the greater rock and took to Babylon. The Dome of the Chain is no more than a spray of Byzantine columns under a canopy: a sad echo, in its subtle, tattered octagon, of the Dome of the Rock for which it served as treasury. The Arabs say that a chain was suspended from heaven there at some early time and used to discover perjurers, for a link of it would fall off in the hand of a liar. But one day a Jew who owed a debt of gold melted the sum into the head of his staff before he was brought to judgment. As he clutched the chain he gave his staff to the plaintiff to hold, then swore that he had returned the money into the hand of his accuser. No link fell away in his fingers, but the chain, with a babble of disgust, vanished forever.

I met a sheikh by the Gate of Darkness.

'I've been living here more than sixty years,' he said, 'and I only know a spoonful of those little domes. Most of them stay locked. But they are all holy! Did you know that Alexander prayed here? And over there Abraham prayed, with his back to us. *Byimkin?* And Omar and Solomon over there.'

He played with the air as if the prophets would materialize at the stab of a finger, talking with a distant intentness, the words falling rounded from little bow-shaped lips. The whole *Haram*, in his imagination, was filled with the comings and goings of saints and warriors.

'And Mahomet prayed by that other little dome, then walked to the rock to go up to heaven, leaving his mare, the Lightning, behind – may God sustain him! – and climbing up by ladder.' He smiled through the drizzle of his beard.

'And what was the Lightning like?'

'*Ktir letif*. Fat.'

'Fat?'

'Yes. In good condition. Otherwise, how could she have come all that way? From Mecca to Medinah in a few minutes? I saw a picture of her once – may God forgive me! – and she was . . . fat!

And the rock, as Mahomet ascended, hovered a little above the earth. Light as a little girl! And it is still in the air.'

I said that I had seen the rock and that it did not appear to be in the air.

'It *used* to be in the air. But it terrified everybody. Pregnant women lost their babies at the sight of it! So the sultan, wanting to keep up the population, built the hillside higher under it. And now it is attached! That is why it is the highest part of the *Haram* and the Aqsa is so far below.'

The Aqsa, the Farthest Mosque, spread its luxuriant body by the *Haram*'s south wall. Walid, mightiest of caliphs, completed the first mosque early in the eighth century, but nothing remains except a few columns in the east. It was raised as the mosque of the *Haram es-Sherif* – for the Dome of the Rock is not a mosque, but a shrine – and five thousand people can worship among its columns. Deep and sternly aisled, like the earliest Syrian churches, the Knights Templars used it as a palace in Crusading years and stabled their horses in the vaults nearby. Their 'armoury' still runs through the Women's Mosque and through a part of the museum beyond it, its glades of arches naked and white.

In the mosque, through many generations, the ghost of Rome remained – the trabeate aisles whose wooden beams remembered the forest-darkened hills of Byzantine and earlier years. The eleventh-century Fatimids had restored the building stoutly, and the arches of the dome are theirs, and the tambour above. Under the porticoed arcade, vaguely Romanesque, Israeli troops had blown in a door to enter. Far on every side the aisles were borne immaculate and clinical on vast Carrara columns, the gift of Mussolini. They spread in seven valleys on a lake of mulberry carpets, brilliant in their paleness, and over their cross-beams and arcades the wooden ceilings sent by King Farouk shone exquisite in gold and blue.

All this was modern or its age concealed, but led as if by chance to the sanctuary's ancient heart. Mosaic plants leant out like fans, and the drum of the cupola held medieval green and golden urns. It was as if alone in all the shrine this old and glimmering dome held life – for the feeling of life is a quality of beauty – and that the aisles were only the spastic limbs of its jewelled body.

There was a fine *mihrab* – the prayer-niche which points to

Mecca – and two others to the west, dedicated to Moses and Jesus. A cedar-wood pulpit stood in the dark, carved even to the panels of its steeply climbing stair: a masterpiece in Damascene, jointed without nails, and chastely inlaid in ivory and mother-of-pearl. Nureddine, sultan of Damascus, commissioned it in Aleppo as a pledge that he would recapture Jerusalem; and Saladin, his successor, set it in the Aqsa when the city fell.

Where men imagined Omar's mosque had been, a shrine in the south-east is named after him, holding a *mihrab* of twisted, intestinal columns, and a view of sunburnt valleys to the south. The Templars had a chapel in a sanctuary nearby, lit through a rose-window, and the Moslems set it later with another *mihrab*, more beautiful, named after Zachariah, a mongrel Moslem saint compounded from the Bible.

These, and the aged columns round them, lay close about the chancel's shining walls. I looked up and saw the cupola, carved and painted in the eleventh century – a time of vanished beauty – and restored by Saladin. Its patterns ripple out exquisitely, overlapping like fish's scales, and all its tints are subtle bronze and silver, the shimmered colours of a fading year. It is, perhaps, the finest of the city's domes, but this autumnal loveliness dwindles to modern piers, so ancient and elusive does beauty's secret seem to be.

I returned down the long aisles and trod unknowing over the stone-flagged 'Grave of the Sons of Aaron', where two of the murderers of Thomas à Becket may lie; for Hoveden writes that they asked penance of Pope Alexander III, who sent them to the Holy Land, and 'they died at Montenegro, and were buried at Jerusalem before the doors of the Temple' (Roger Hoveden, d. 1201, *Cronica*).

Outside the sun was softened in haze and a wind touched the nettle trees. By the Dome of the Rock a Jewish guide was describing to tourists the site in the time of Solomon; but they stood unlistening, dazed in its present beauty: the first and most perfect shrine in Islam.

One might suppose, if no history was written, that the nomad had come from the south inspired by some composite view of life and realized here, perfect and beautiful for ever, the vision of his wanderings. Astonished by what they had done, the Arabs later assigned the whole sanctuary to the work of *djinns*. In earliest times, they said, its courts held fifty gates and flared with five thousand lamps. A chain was suspended above the rock and held 'the horns from the ram which Abraham sacrificed' and the diadem of Chosroes, King of Kings. In the days of 'Abd-el-Malik it was elaborate with ceremonial. Every Monday and Thursday silken curtains were drawn along arcades to screen the rock, where saffron was heaped and soaked all night with ambergris, rosewater and musk. At morning the servants washed their feet and hands in perfume at the rock and walked upon it holding gold and silver censers. The dome grew misty with the redolence of aloes, the silken curtains were drawn away, and like a salvo of aromatic cannon-smoke the incense-clouds rolled through the doors and into the markets, while the voice of muezzins bade the people pray.

The only bouquet left was the half-scent of the pines. But Eden, says legend, is closer here than anywhere on earth. Moslems believe that a certain man, descending the Well of the Leaf, wandered by chance into the garden of paradise. He plucked a leaf and stuck it, Arab-fashion, behind his ear before returning, and it never withered. The Eden which he saw was the desert-warrior's elysium of shadow-stained waters and cow-eyed houris, a pastoral New Jerusalem; for 'in lovely gardens shall the faithful dwell in bliss' (Koran 52).

Afterwards many others came and peered into the well to glimpse the lost paradise, and saw themselves reflected. But the secret way was never found again.

II

The Years of Islam

The worst of men is he whose today falls short of his yesterday.
(MAQAMAT HARIRI)

Of the four centuries between the raising of the Dome and the coming of the Crusaders, scarcely a building in Jerusalem remains. The caliphs ruled her distantly from Baghdad and Charlemagne's protection grew weak in his descendants as their empire was shivered away. The Byzantines under Nicephorus Phocas, marching to within sight of the holy walls, retired when their soldier-emperor died, and soon after, in 969, the city was taken by the Fatimid Arabs, who had set up a rival caliphate in Cairo. Mukaddasi, a native of Jerusalem, speaks of injustice, dirt and high prices, and complains that Jews and Christians occupied many positions of influence; but by this time the Moslem population was dominant, and in 1007 the lieutenant of the mad caliph Hakim pulled down much of the Church of the Holy Sepulchre, and 'persevered in destroying the Sacred Tomb, to the last vestige, and hacked out a great piece of it, and took it away' (Yahia of Antioch).

Seventy years later the Seljuk Turks captured the city, and their barbarian law was one of many motives which brought the First Crusade on its long march southward. Commerce, politics, and adventure have long ago taken their place beside the romantic view that the Crusades were a purely pious enterprise, but William of Tyre, who judged his contemporaries shrewdly, describes an upsurge of passion as the knights drew near the city. They fell on their knees, flung off their shoes and kissed the dust, and their leaders have passed beyond history into the spirit of *chansons de geste*, of the chivalric ideal itself: the knight *sans peur et sans reproche*. In June 1099 Godfrey de Bouillon, Robert of Normandy, Tancred, Baldwin and Raymond of Toulouse spread their camp before the northern walls of a city which the Fatimids had recaptured and refortified the year before, and stormed them in mid-July. The Jews were burnt in their synagogues, the Moslems slain by thousands in the streets, until no enemy remained, and at evening the soldiers 'exchanged fresh clothes for those which were blood-stained, and walked barefoot with sighs and tears through the holy places of the city where the Saviour Jesus Christ had trodden as a man, and sweetly kissed the ground which his feet had touched' (William of Tyre, *Godeffroy of Boloyne*).

Godfrey de Bouillon was elected king, but refused to wear a crown of gold where the Saviour had endured a crown of thorns, and assumed the simple title of 'Defender of the Holy Sepulchre'. For eighty-eight years the Crusaders were to hold Jerusalem, while their kings grew steadily more oriental and less commanding, the courts crowded with Lebanese doctors and Syrian sages, and softened by the silks and wines of Damascus.

South of the Holy Sepulchre an emptiness chills the streets. They grow short and wide under pretentious nineteenth-century arches, and criss-cross in an orderly, heartless manner among the shops of Armenian jewellers. In the eleventh century merchants from Amalfi built a chapel here, a hospital named from St John the Almoner, a Benedictine abbey and a monastery-church. They tended the Crusader wounded when the city was taken, and many of the casualties, remembering their charity, joined the Order of the Hospital until it had grown into a military brotherhood.

The compound swelled to a giant square, where the Hospitallers' bazaars ran and caravanserais clustered in columned courts. Even after the Crusaders had gone it remained a medical centre, and Arabs, in remembrance or contempt, still call it the Muristan, 'the Hospital' or 'Lunatic Asylum'. Years later it began to disintegrate and the Ottomans used the bossed stones in their ramparts; a seventeenth-century pilgrim said that 'one sees still their infirmaries, and other rooms; but everything is abandoned, and nobody appears to live there' (Père Nau, *Voyage Nouveau*). The Greek Orthodox bought half the site and demolished history and beauty, while St Mary Latin, the Benedictine abbey, was smothered by the German Church of the Redeemer.

The calmness of the Muristan is an enigma in the crush and shouting. The foolish arches and the breadth of the streets are a leftover from Ottoman 'improvements' which mercifully failed, and a banal fountain stands on the site of the monastery-church.

'Is it not splendid?' cried a storekeeper. 'The arches, the cleanness, the openness! I thank God for it.'

I saw no reason why he should blame God, who had little say in the decisions of the Sublime Porte.

'But believe me, *Howadja*, the old here is disgusting. You see the Redeemer Church, the German one?'

I nodded.

'I have not been inside,' he said, 'but I believe that inside it is *old*. You are *tooriste* so that will please you. It is as old as Omar, perhaps as old as Solomon! Perhaps . . .'

We entered a modern doorway, climbed a few steps and found ourselves in the two-tiered cloisters of St Mary Latin, walking in coolness down the deep Crusader strength which keeps its beauty, like a well-boned face, even in decay.

'How old?' asked the storekeeper.

'Twelfth century in Christian time.'

'How old is that? Omar?'

'Saladin.' (Local Arab ages are generally graded 'Solomon', 'Omar', 'Saladin', 'New-and-Magnificent'.)

Below us the courtyard lay protected in the aisles of its quietness, pale galleries of sobriety and silence. Buddleia and lilac spilt over the stone, and troughs were spaced among the pillars, where flowers grew lightly out of the watered earth. The sense of peace was heavy as a fragrance. In a court a garden lay with ancient fragments scattered about, and descending to the lower gallery I saw Byzantine capitals used again from the first church. Under a sad fall of ivy the medieval stones were thronged in many arches, grown with a static grace from one another's shoulders. Lilac without butterflies, ivy without owls – even the cloistered flowers were held in a windless calm, the trance of slow monastic days, forgotten monks and silent bells.

From their short kingdom the Crusaders left much behind. They built as if their world would last for ever, laying stones massive and smooth-rimmed in defence, churches like castles, whose deep windows guide in light as if it were a fluid. They were, perhaps, the first to raise the small domed houses in Jerusalem, and there is a ruined church to St Abraham in a fallen outwork by the Damascus Gate, its frescos warm on a dado where the Tartars pulled it down; and the church of St James the Severed, now a mosque of white-washed stone where porters pray. East of the Muristan are twelfth-century *suqs*, fresh-smelling mounds of fruit and vegetables which glisten in Crusader halls. Two passageways, each a hundred yards long, slide narrow and intimate under high vaults, cluttered with clothes and a miscellany of shops; and a third is filled with black-smiths and vegetable-sellers, sick with banging and tinkling and rasping, the rush of lost chickens and the blue flash of foundry flames. In Crusader times the *suqs* were called Street of Herbs and Covered Street and the Street of Bad Cookery, and here and there, but difficult to find, an inscribed T marks the old estate of the Templars or a 'Scta Anna', the property of St Anne's.

My Polish hospice had belonged to Hungarians in Crusader years, though only their mellow floors remained, and sometimes at evening, seeing the feudal mass of La Grande with a watering-can among the shrubs, I could imagine that time was folding up.

'You are not growing!' she would tell the flowers menacingly. 'Come! Grow!'

Jerusalem's loveliest church, the Crusader St Anne's, rises from a garden of pepper and acacia trees where White Fathers amble drowsily in prayer. A fortress-shrine for soldier-priests and kings, it stands in greyed stone consecrating a place old in Byzantine tradition, where St Anne, the Virgin's mother, had lived and given birth to her child. Its windows are high and few and its door simple, mounted by plain Burgundian arches.

Saladin turned it to a religious school after the reconquest, and his inscription is still above the door. 'All the blessings ye enjoy come from God! This *madrasah* has been founded by the triumphant lord, Salah-ed-Din . . .' But the Christian aura remained, and in the eighteenth century the Moslems abandoned it, saying that ghosts shrieked there; they offered the keys to the Franciscans, who refused them, and the church declined. In 1842 the Moslems hoped to rebuild it as a school, but their masons were Christians from Bethlehem, who were anxious that Islam should not profane the site, and worked so slowly, tipping the stones into cisterns, that it was never finished. The governor quartered his cavalry in the falling aisles, and caravans covered it with the filth of camels, until at the end of the Crimean War it was given to the French, who restored it finely.

Although crumbling where Israeli shells have struck, it is still noble in the starkness of its lines. A high apse and a drumless dome are dim at the back of its austerity, and down the aisles the vastness of the piers grows airy, blossomed to vaults whose ribs are lined in whiter stone. Dry, poor Carolingian capitals, left from the earlier church, go unnoticed in the weight of the pillars, and the deep Crusader windows are latticed to a shrivelled spray of light.

I descended to the grotto-crypt of the Virgin's Nativity – a warren which the Byzantines cut clean; but little is left and the dignity, the touch on truth, was suddenly gone. I climbed out of its baroque into the upper church, wandered round the precincts of the White Fathers who keep a seminary and museum, and sat under the smooth limbs of a jacaranda tree.

Beside me the ground had collapsed in ruin. It was as if the bombs which had spattered the church had fallen in a dense, mysterious rain on this half-acre and opened up the century-filled veins of the earth. Here in the time of Christ lay the Piscina Probatica – the Pond of the Sheep Gate – and the tombstone of a deacon of the 'church of the Probaticum' stood nearby. 'There is at Jerusalem,' says St John's Gospel, 'by the sheep market a pool, which is called in the Hebrew tongue Bethesda, having five porches. In these lay a great multitude of impotent folk, of blind, halt, withered, waiting for the moving of the water. For an angel went down at a certain season into the pool, and troubled the water: whosoever then first after the troubling of the water stepped in was made whole of whatsoever disease he had' (John 5:2–4).

The bases of columns were gathered round the lip of the dead pond, and left imagined porticoes in banks of ruin. A colonnade had divided the reservoir gracefully more than a century before Christ, and the barrage was there still, pierced by a passageway between the lakes, and falling to waters shrunk in a dark calm.

I descended into the ruins where a White Father guided me, bustling round fitful walls. Here Christ healed with a word the paralytic man who had lain by the water unable to reach it before 'another steppeth down'. Baths were scooped in rock where a crowd of pagan gods had been invoked for healing, and the pools, it seems, were linked to the Gihon fountain underground and rose and fell with it, so that the Jews assigned their trembling to a water-troubling angel and made the cult respectable.

Along the fifth portico the empress Eudocia built a church, poised like a ship on the waters. Its walls lay about in loosened ridges, and columns had left their rose-coloured plinths in the east, kept new by the earth with the crosses clear upon them. Baths and cisterns, closed beneath church floors, now opened again to dislocated fingers of light, and a paving of grey-veined marble ran delicately in and out of dust.

On these Byzantine ruins the Crusaders built anew, but only their church's apse remains, ugly and broken in the sky. Far down, snapped columns were green under the water and a single arch, tall where the lake had fostered it, lifted lightly from the rubble. The White Father left me, his sandals flapping brusquely on the paths, and I went again through the geometry of ruins, imagining the porticoes where they spread under the dust, and the hideous obstacle-race of the sick, groping to reach the rippled waters first.

There was no massacre when the Moslems retook Jerusalem, and Saladin, it is said, wept when he saw the bereaved Crusader women, and released many with his own hand. In 1229 Frederick II, the excommunicated emperor of Germany, regained the city by treaty, walked into the Holy Sepulchre and laconically crowned himself king: 'Well, I said I would come here, and here I am.' But in 1244 the mercenary Tartars of the sultan in Cairo ravaged the city, and the slave-kings of Egypt, the Mamelukes, settled down a few years later to a rule of nearly three centuries.

The *Haram es-Sherif* is lined by their religious schools, the *madrasahs*, and their tombs. They stand among its walls and by its gates, each entranceway mellow and withdrawn, set in variegated courses under a high, stalactic porch: lost aristocrats, the iron plates peeling from their doors, the dovetailed decorations rattled loose by time, inscriptions worn to wrinkles. The Othmaniye is no more than a ruined terrace, about whose falling arches children play, and by the Gate of Darkness the blazon of the *djukander*, the polo-master to the sultan, has outlived the halls he built. Saladin himself perched a *madrasah* on the Gate of the Chain, and beside it the Ashrafiyeh is fiercely-elaborate in the alternating yellow and rose of its entrance; but it leads only to a shell, to gates and windows lost in pastel walls, and the quaintly vaulted stairway of a minaret.

The school of Tingiz is by the Chain Gate, with the sultan's heraldic cups above the doors. Here the Ottomans held tribunal in the four-bayed hall, and the Sanhedrin met in the time of Christ, who may have stood upon the few Roman slabs remaining. Beyond is the tomb of an unknown princess and the pretty, jaded Kalidi library, with grass-sown graves in its courtyard and the cenotaph of a Qaresmian Tartar chief surrounded by book-shelves. And in the Aqabat et-Tekiyeh rises the severe and splendid palace of the Lady Tonsuq with her tomb opposite, neglected now, and littered with the horns of slaughtered bullocks.

The past has grown too massive for its people, who live in it as birds inhabit castles, forgetful of its meanings and impervious to its glory. Most of the buildings are only theatre, and the debating of the great religious schools is unimaginable in halls piled with rubble, nests of cats and cluttered rooms. Inside is nothing but a chaos of poor dwellings round musty stairs.

The caravanserais were always fewer than in the merchant cities of Syria, and are half-empty – the Oil Khan a museum, the Khan es Sultan wrapped in a weft of dirt and flies; and although the stables remain, with balconies upheld on curling, medieval consoles, the ancient tracks are gone which gave them life. Only the Suq Qattanin – the Cotton Market – outshines its own dilapidation where the light flows in moonbeams through a dust-hazed air, and a few people live or work in darkened corridors. The vaults reach back a hundred yards to the spiked gate of Tingiz, but only a bath – the Hamam es Schlifa – is left, with a deep and curious spring which Moslems say flows underground from Arabia, for women have found there the jewelry which they lost in Mecca's holy well.

When Selim the Grim took Jerusalem in 1517 the city had long been in decline. For a while the Ottomans administered her well, and Suleiman the Magnificent built her circlet of walls – a gesture of prestige more than of defence – endowed her with fountains and repaired her aqueducts.

Then began the long stagnation. Cut off by brigands from the regional capital, Damascus, Jerusalem was isolated under despotic governors who would be removed by a suspicious sultan if their administration became effective. Wealth and enterprise were taxed away, and the population declined. To European travellers this desolation was romantic, and they portrayed a city of dreamy, lithographic beauty, shrub-cascaded palaces and pastoral Arabs lolled in Arcadian ruins. Yet even in the nineteenth century, when greater pilgrimage and foreign missions revived a little wealth, Chateaubriand wrote that the houses were 'like prisons or sepulchres' and Edward Lear, who came to sketch, called Jerusalem 'the odiousest place on earth'. The civil service lived on bribery; false witnesses were a vital adjunct to the courts; and the soldiery consisted of Bashi Bazouks, a kind of mounted banditry, who conscripted the garrison by capturing peasants in the countryside; and those who were caught served for five or seven years and earned six shillings and eightpence a year, which was not often paid.

'We were seated all day in front of the principal gates of Jerusalem', wrote Lamartine; 'we made the circuit of the walls in passing before all its other gates. No one entered, no one came out; the beggar even was not seated in the gateway; the sentinel did not show himself on its post . . . We saw but four funeral parties issue in silence from the Damascus Gate.'

'Before everything I see I feel emptier than a hollow cask', recorded Flaubert, disillusioned long before he reached the city. 'This morning, in the Holy Sepulchre, a dog would have been more moved than I. Whose fault is it, merciful Lord? Theirs? Yours? Or mine? Theirs, I believe, mine next, yours above all. But how false everything is! How they lie! How it is all whitewashed, veneered, polished, used for exploitation, propaganda and the customer! Jerusalem is a walled charnel house.'

The Ottomans built little of distinction, except the public kitchen set up by Sultana Roxelana, the cruel and lovely 'Joyous One' of Suleiman the Magnificent. But the city walls, of course, were his, weathered grey or tawny as the wind has chosen, and like a ship they plunge and rise in the land's waves, heavy with towers. The Moslems say that they were built by two brothers, who started from the Jaffa Gate and circled away from one another's sight for seven years until they met at the Gate of St Stephen; but because they excluded from their walls the Tomb of David, runs the legend, the sultan had them hanged, and buried them by the Jaffa Gate in the two white graves which lie under a fig tree.

The seven gates have taken many names. Several are small and functional – the New Gate, the Dung Gate and Herod's Gate, once called the Gate of Flowers. The Damascus Gate is the showpiece of the walls – an exuberant symbol of power – built where every age since Herod Agrippa has known an entranceway. The bullet-scraped Gate of Sion bends through a fine tower, as does the Jaffa Gate where the wall was battered down to let in Kaiser Wilhelm with pomp.

Compact on the crest of the eastern hill, St Stephen's Gate was pierced by the Israelis in 1967 and a leaf of its iron door cast aside; but the portal itself is complete, with jaunty crenellations and the moulded lions of Baibars torn from some other building. Lions of the podgy Moslem kind, the people round about have an affection for them, and say that they pounced on the Turkish sultan in a dream and persuaded him to build their walls.

Rarely were the walls defended. Suleiman, who owned the best artillery in the world, must have known that they were proof only against roving tribesmen; but they saw no true army until General Allenby passed through on foot with the first Christian force to enter the city for seven hundred years. Jerusalem was heaved out of stagnation and into the civil discords of the British mandate.

'Our city has always suffered for its holiness. Holiness is its tragedy. Perhaps that is why our people are unhappier than others. They can remember nothing but struggles. Blood. They have been harmed by this sanctity more than they have benefited. I myself remember . . .'

He was an old man, Aref el Aref, seated in a study full of aging books; but a littered desk betrayed activity, and out of the boneless velour of his face the mouth was amused and articulate. He had lived seventy-seven years of Jerusalem's history, and reflected its fervour and sadness. Conscripted by the Turks in the First World War, he had been captured by the Russians at Erzerum and became one of the few men to escape from Siberia, journeying to Vladivostock in the hope of joining the Arab revolt in the Hejaz. By the time he returned the war was over, and in 1920 the British government accused him of leading riots against increasing Jewish immigration, and condemned him to death; but the High Commissioner commuted the sentence to imprisonment, and he escaped to the tribes of the Moab hills, eluding all attempts at capture.

The thought amused him now. From time to time he rose to draw a book from his shelves and verify some point of history. He appeared to regard the British without bitterness, for he had gained a pardon, become a mandatory official, mayor of Jerusalem, and was decorated for services to the Empire. Above all he had known the growth of Arab nationalism and had been its instrument.

'I was one of the leaders of a demonstration of forty thousand Moslems and Christians against the British. We went round all the consulates. Ten speeches a day! I stood holding the hand of a Christian and shouted "I am a Moslem. My brother is a Christian. We no longer fight. We are children of our country and the past is forgotten."'

Jerusalem was his passion, his native city. 'In the 1948 war Jerusalem suffered more than any other place. Even in this last war four hundred were killed. It is a hard place. Bitter. There is little water and not much arable land. Yet people have to live. They cannot fill their stomachs with religion.' He stabbed with his fingers, as if pinning down the truth as it flew by. 'This is why Moslems here are sometimes austere. They rarely drink and you don't hear much music. There is scarcely a prostitute in the place and a few women still wear the veil. I think we are more temperate too in our loves and hates. It is said we have *Helem*, that we are not excitable. But we are desperately devoted. Scarcely anybody emigrates. Whereas in Bethlehem and Ramallah for instance . . . half Ramallah is in America!'

'Those who leave Jerusalem,' I said, 'must feel that they are leaving the centre of the world.'

'The *Sakhra*, yes – the rock beneath the Dome – this is indeed the world's centre. We say that *al-Yom* – the Last Day – will be inaugurated there; that Jerusalem will be a part of *al-Aher*, of paradise. It has been promised, and may God will it.' His fingers struck down at the table with force. 'There's an irony for you! Jerusalem a paradise!'

★

A faith more realistic than most, Islam fed the roots of an early society, just and broadly democratic, and its law has remained the basis for civil legislation today. But a religion serving a community may age quicker than a faith which fosters the soul. Some plasticity, an ultimate depth, is lost, and as the Jews' Talmud has overlaid the Law, and the Church the Bible, so the Hadith, the traditional sayings of the Prophet, have become almost as revered as the Koran. Islam has often grown hard and formal, and with it the social structure has atrophied, society itself fallen asleep. A race evolves its own rule of life and perhaps deserves the government, the society and the religion which it forms; but it may happen that a people's chance for growth is stifled by the bonds which its fathers set upon it, and that the new spirit, in its first weakness, is locked in embryo for centuries.

Christianity, which treated the individual, was shunned for the blasphemy that God could have a son by a mortal woman, and its Trinity revolted the old concept of the One God. 'I testify that there is no God but God,' calls the muezzin, and exorcises, as he does so, the legion spirits of his pagan past. The Christian Father is not there, nor the Great Confessor. The Moslem Deity is the Compassionate, the Merciful, the Patient; not often the God of active love. From His impersonal vastness and the rigid forms adopted by His faithful, the Sufis, the mystics of Islam, turned away. They felt the everlasting compulsion, in religion or society, to slip the bonds of orthodoxy and swim into some freer element toward the reality or the illusion of a closer truth.

The Crusader church of St Agnes, given as a mosque to Persian mystics, is still pretty and modest with a narrow entrance unproclaimed and bare white walls. Years ago Mevlevi dervishes, who whirled there to hypnotic music, became lost in some world of which they could not speak, their dance symbolic of the planets turning in heaven, their souls diffused into the all-pervading unity of God.

There were other mystics in the Madrasah Bakriyah and in the Kankah Mosque where the Crusader Patriarchs had a palace, but their gardens and rooms of contemplation have been turned to other uses and the Sufis are dying away. They meet only quietly, often in secret. Like the Confucians before them, they credit their master with a mysticism which he despised or never knew, and orthodox Islam, which of all great religions is the most simply practical, is wary of its mystics.

I was told that Sufis still lived in Jerusalem, a secret sect which had come from Bokhara in Turkestan; and walking down the Via Dolorosa one day, I saw a Mongol face like a benevolent moon setting over a cup of coffee. The café turned out to be the centre of the tiny sect of Nachshbandiyeh, 'the Carving on the Rock'.

Its sheikh said with kindness that he could tell me nothing of his people's worship, but after we had been talking for a while about the love of a man for a woman, he became less guarded: 'When you love a girl you see only her. Her face is always in your eyes. So it is with God. Love is the shadow of God.' In Sufism it is an old belief that love for a woman may open the way to love for the Divine. 'In Islam, you know, we don't believe in the monastery. We take what is beautiful in the world because it is God's; the natural cannot be despised.'

I remained silent, for this is not the tradition of Islam but that of Sufism. He smiled: a man with a white-tipped beard, half-grown, and a lean face in which the eyes stood brilliantly, deep and assured, like instruments of thought and speaking.

The world, said a great Sufi, is the 'breath of the Merciful' (Ibn el Arabi), and the mystics do not turn from it in the Indian way, but recognize its godliness. They love and marry and enjoy the peace of rivers and gardens, and although they may find a discipline in poverty and solitude, their goal is *fana*, the ecstatic union which dissolves the frontier between God and His creation. The old order slips away. The dictatorship of Allah mellows to the transcendence of the good. Man grows in stature, his soul divine, and love and repentance, which together cleanse his sight of God, are exalted to an everyday concern.

'If my son has done wrong,' said the sheikh, 'our relationship is broken. His heart is closed. But if he approaches me in uprightness of soul, we meet truly and may talk. That is how we should meet God, for sin is a severance. Anything which cuts off man from God is a sin, the only sin. War severs. All untruth and thoughtlessness sever.' He bowed his head in regret. Some underlying inheritance linked him to the Russian nun at Bethany. 'I am sad for Jerusalem.

Some have gone away, even of our brotherhood. Many are angry. Who would have thought that men are rooted deep in God? The ways of gentleness are forgotten.'

He showed me the robes of his sect, the striped coats with their wide, tapering sleeves, and the quadrangular caps of Bokhara. He talked of the Mevlevi, the Whirling Dervishes, and of the Howling Dervishes who had swallowed glass and snakes.

'But they have disappeared from here. Their actions were useless. How will I approach my Maker through dancing or eating snakes? No. I will reach Him by thought and right living. Our movement has produced many just men, men of reputation.' Each week, he confided, they met and sat in the darkness of the room and contemplated God with lanterns burning before them – 'darkness lifts the mind to the One'. It was a way of discipline, of inner rest, and of a further secret, a sublimity of which he could not speak, for to describe in words the last phase of the mystic experience would be like annotating music by an arrangement of stones.

He told me to be careful in the city. Nothing was as happy as it had been. Everything was changing, he said, all over the world. 'And my son will not carry on my ways.'

12

The Two Cities

The broken string may be joined, but a knot will always remain.

(ANWAR-I-SUHEILI)

The legend-histories of Jew and Arab say that in a remote time their two peoples knew a common origin, sprung from Isaac and Ishmael, the sons of Abraham; and certainly they are of kindred race, however strangely mixed in later years, and their wars and jealousies are those of brothers. In early centuries the Moslems were generally tolerant of the Jews, whose manner and appearance were as oriental as theirs, and lived with them peacefully while Europe was steeped in persecution. Only since Israel returned in half-Western guise has a consistent hatred developed, and now that the barbed-wire barriers have gone from Jerusalem, these two worlds – the Israeli and the Arab – know divisions more subtle and profound.

The Arab city within the walls is Jerusalem in essence. A hundred years ago there was almost nothing outside. It is the mountain-town of the Mamelukes and Ottomans still, stone-flagged slopes and valleys white with sun, streets thin and confused, mellow as hill-lanes of Umbria or Provence. The walls rise secret on every side. Doors open onto no Damascene courtyards of flying stairs. Suleiman's lovely fountains have run dry. The camel-coloured stone, the quaint arches and many steps where scarcely a mule will go – all beauty beats against a time-sanctioned feudal squalor, overcrowding, dirt, malnutrition.

The city is bowed with age, even the children puckered, the population almost all Palestinians, with many refugees. Not one in ten is sound in body. On the lane beneath my window half the footfalls seemed to limp, and ten times a day I would hear clicking sticks, as blind men felt their way with uncanny sureness over the steps.

Jerusalem works, one way or another, in the service of religion, and when the pilgrims fail, the people are poor. Before five o'clock in the morning the country women sit in the streets with their fruit – sturdy, listless girls. Hens are taken from place to place in wicker cages, from which their dismayed white faces and pulsing throats poke out stupidly; and two hours later the whole town is awake.

The mildness of emotion which other Arabs detect in the people, the austerity, even sourness, may be the fruit of disillusion. The Arab lives by his Odyssean cunning; if it fails he starves; but he is quickly shamed into a blaze of violent pride or a spontaneous gift. His friendship may be indiscriminate, his protestations child-like, but trespass a little further on his affections and he is happy to be liked and generous to the point of idiocy.

Yet Jerusalem is unique. There is a bitterness, a cruelty, too elusive to define. Traveller after traveller has noted it. Her surroundings must have spawned it on the people – Judean rock and sand – for the voluptuous sense is lacking which tints the inland cities of Syria. An ascetic element has intruded, an intolerance, and if the Arab is less fervent here, he is also more inured to pain, his own and others', and more abstinent.

All his vernacular qualities are present: the effervescence, the secretiveness and suspicion, the sociability and old-world politesse. In the cafés the faces sucking their narghilyes have been set by time and chance to incarnate humours. The passion for politics is pared to a sharper scepticism. There is a love of ideas, often without logic; but the visual, Levantine ideality is theirs, so vivid that a man can pluck off the petals of an imaginary flower, or see an absent friend's face clearly enough to nod at it.

Abstract concepts, objective truths, pall before this continent of the senses. A man lives in the sight of his world, often flamboyantly, and he hates to be alone. His emotions are more valid than the vague legions of fact, which may be shuffled around his feelings to satisfy or sanction them. He speaks rather than listens, and gives more gracefully than he receives.

The backdrop of his life, especially in Jerusalem, is deeply conservative. The family, tentacled and patriarchal, sustains and burdens every man. In prouder days it was dishonourable for a man to work for others; his ideal, in fancy, was the Bedouin cavalier, riding insolently among his servants, and the Moslem habit of wearing pyjamas until late into the morning is, I believe, a symbol of this superiority over environment. There is still an unblushing love of leisure, both as status and as enjoyment, and the chronic industriousness of the West appals him.

A man used to inherit his business through many ancestors, and Jerusalem is a city of these immemorial families, craftsmen and aristocrats, some of whom claim to trace their forefathers to the years of Omar. But the old patterns are fragmenting, and a son may now ignore his father's trade and search for a better position; the Husseinis are no longer in sole charge of religious affairs, nor the Nashashibis dominant in municipal office. A single generation has deserted the paths of centuries.

The modern Arab quarters outside the walls, built pleasantly in limestone, are an emblem of this change. The Palestine Archaeological, or Rockefeller, Museum is here, overlooking the walls from the north-east where Robert of Normandy had camped in 1099 and invaders from many ages found the city vulnerable.

The museum is rich in the earliest years of man, and is famous for its Dead Sea Scrolls, temporarily removed, for the Galilee skull and the Mount Carmel skeleton a hundred thousand years old, still hunched as he was found. Here was the simple paraphernalia of Chalcolithic people, groping over centuries to a vestige of luxury: the barbs of their fishing-hooks keener, the beads of their necklaces more polished. By the second millennium jewellery appears, delicate and golden, and painted birds are walking awkwardly across the decorated flasks, with fish and straw-legged deer. Then the late Iron Age brings a warmth of recognition: the puppets and symbols grown human, the proportions gayer – with the glass of Rome filmed by time to an iridescence more lovely than its makers intended.

There were stucco mouldings from the eighth-century palace of the caliph Hisham near Jericho – decorations which covered walls, arches, ceilings, columns – eclectic and fastidious. Many wide-eyed, mythic creatures had once scrambled over soffits and lintels to the outrage of the Islamic orthodox, and were propped up in fragments. Most outrageous were the gauche, Hindu-like figures, whose fat, splayed arms upheld whole cornices. Eyes popped, beards jutted, lips grimaced, and women with over-tended hair flaunted exorbitant breasts and wrinkled stomachs.

At the end of the North Gallery I was halted by the restoration of a Hyksos family tomb – a little community dwindled to nothingness, its bowls and jugs all turning to the same scattered pallor like the chalk of crumpled seashells.

I passed to cloisters into the light of Greece and the sun. A pretty Armenian girl was reading among the flowers. A few capitals lay around a pool flecked with tomato-coloured goldfish, and over a marble sarcophagus, in dazzling violence, rushed Greeks and Amazons to battle.

Since the time of Hadrian the spine of the Old City has been the Khan es Zeit, which runs from the Damascus Gate to the medieval *suqs* by spice and pastry stalls, and shops with fruit and sacks of musky nuts. These are the open counters of the orient, whose covers roll up to their lintels and are unfolded at the rumour of a riot. Boys struggle with strange burdens and tourists lose each other in cheerless-looking knots among the thrust of donkeys.

The markets trickling in coloured glades to David Street are those which the Crusaders built, and beyond them are others, shadowed and chaotic, which lend their wares a chance glamour. Sheep are tethered to anything at hand, and mottled hens lie in heaps, their feet bound under them. The vendor sits unsmiling by his store, or shouts suddenly. The alternate clamour and whispered confabulation of a bargain are more like an orchestra than a debate .

Only the costume of the peasants is old. The swagger of the *keffiyeh* is everywhere, and the grace of the white head-veil and long, embroidered dress. Under the woman's headcloth, and the gold coins which were her husband's gift, are the classic, narrow north Arabian faces – the eagle nose, retreating forehead and chin. Their jewellery is not often seen, for the rustic arts are dying and the Bedouin and village silversmith is almost gone. Rare are the amulets and phylacteries, the long tasselled brooches and amber necklaces with bells to warn off demons – all the old chattels of a *djinn*-fearing woman.

The city's sanctity has helped to debauch its art, for a tawdry souvenir of Jerusalem may be sold on sentiment alone. Tourist bric-à-brac is smothered in mother-of-pearl or carved out of olive without thought to the humour of its heavily grained wood. The business of making 'ancient ikons' flourishes. To the end of Ottoman times artist-pilgrims painted them for wealthy families in return for lodging, but their works, and those which the monasteries sold, are vanishing.

In 1919 a few Armenians were brought from Turkey to redecorate the Dome of the Rock, and their sons – quiet, serious men – still work in pottery and copy graceful tiles from those in churches. Armenian jewellers rarely mass-produce as they do in Syria but fulfil individual orders; and their work is subtle and demanding. The solid peasant jewellery is still for sale, and I have seen antique Damascus silver, with copper from Iran and Syria.

But for the rest, the old flair has gone. The Arab idles in the sunshine of his past. Strolling in the city's self-tormented sleep, one sees him sitting on the stones which his fathers cut, and wonders where the genius of the great builders of Baghdad and Cordoba went, Averroës and Avicenna, the *Prolegomena* of Ibn-Khaldun, the *Meditations* of Ma 'arri.

From the thirteenth century until a few years ago the Moslem spring pilgrimage was immense on the road to Jericho. Moses, declared medieval sages, was carried there by angels from his lonely grave in the Moab hills; and although Baibars inaugurated the myth to counteract Christian rites at Easter, the pilgrimage was ardent which has so recently dwindled.

At the Jaffa Gate the ramparts release the old world on the new, the Jewish metropolis. The walled town is suddenly distant: a yellowed tigerish city, a sheet of palisades beyond the prospect of modern Jerusalem.

I went into the open town, walking in an instant from a last generation to the rawness of a race only recently reborn. The charm was gone, the touch on time. Youth, energy – chance notices blazoned its heart: 'Goldstein Youth Village', 'International Culture Centre for Youth', 'Boy's Town'. The young are the symbol of a phoenix people, a nation in danger. Jerusalem, the most conservative of Israel's cities, yet has the greatest proportion of native-born young – the *sabras*, named from the cactus which is prickly outside and soft at heart. They are the new Children of Israel – proud, secular and candid. The conventional, the formal, the polite, are nearly meaningless, and suspect too the spiritual slogans which brought their fathers and grandfathers on the great *Aliya*, the talk of 'Israel's mission' with which Zionist propaganda bored them as children. But their nationalism is as intense as their fathers'; only the God of the holy books has been dethroned; the history, the people and the promised land remain, and the *sabra*'s toughness barely conceals his Jewish sentiment.

The old are different, for they have come from every land in the world, and most of them have suffered. Their intelligence and sophistication are unmatched by material wealth, for they live in small apartments: a classless society without luxury or poverty. The New City was raised in a single century, but its buildings never dominate the people; no faceless, bureaucratic castles line the streets.

Despite their masculine vigour of movement, even the women, whose contrast to the Arab is most marked, show themselves to be of kindred race by their soft, Mediterranean limbs and dark, abundant hair. The features which passed me could scarcely be typified. There were orientals, no different in appearance from the Arabs; and the immemorial faces of European Jewry: the sheltered, olive complexion, the withdrawn paleness and full lips; the long, Aramean look and the short-headed Canaanite.

I left the pleasant suburb of Rehavia for olive-sprinkled valleys, out of whose slopes the future was sprouting in cubes and parterres – the Israel Museum, the Hebrew University – functional, white, defined. This is the New Jerusalem, whose spirit is secular – a lightning growth, sprung out of suffering and diffusion into the youngest democracy in the world.

High to the north the square Knesset, the Parliament, rose from a newly planted wood. The hills poured soft and rounded to Samaria, and a windy butte, the Mount of Joy, marked where Crusader pilgrims first glimpsed the city and a pale mosque hides the legendary tomb of Samuel.

The seven earliest discovered Dead Sea Scrolls are kept among the museum gardens in the Shrine of the Book, beneath a porcelain cupola. A metal cylinder reaches to the apex of the white, striated dome, as if it were whisking a huge, inverted bowl of cream, and underneath, cased in glass, are the tiny, momentous fragments – darkened to slivers. Young people moved around them reverentially, as if in some cathedral to their past, for archaeology uncovers more than knowledge; it feeds the search for identity, their claim to the land, each stone and coin throwing a beam across sixty empty generations to gild the uncertain present with a warmth of belonging.

A garden of modern sculpture was set against the carving of the hills, and the museum spread in terraces of fountains, beautifully ordered: Hannukah lamps, ceremonial instruments and the vestments of the Diaspora – sequined veils from Bokhara, shimmering, stiff Tunisian embroidery and Iranian jewels. I wandered into a seventeenth-century synagogue from Italy – delightful in its harmony of dark, plain woods and the baroque of grey and gold; and into another from Bavaria – a barrel vault painted with animals – and entered the long museum of prehistory, a march of centuries through spacious rooms.

On the other side of the valley, a grass-floored stadium between, was the great Hebrew University; the students are impressive in their quietness and energy and it is, in a sense, the new heart of Israel. A long way to the west, the military dead were buried on Mount Herzl under stone-flagged slopes, and the names of those lost at sea lay upon tombstones beneath a still pool. Lower to the west the memorial of Yad Vashem recorded the six million victims of the Nazi regime. Down the Avenue of the Just the carob trees were green, each planted in gratitude to remember a Gentile's courage. There were archives and a high, concave Pillar of Heroism, a black-floored hall where an everlasting flame played, and a gallery for the paintings of ghetto Jews, worked in a numb, passive trance, as of a people crushed by some unanswerable decree.

All was austere and uncrying, without the isolated horror of the Mount Sion sanctuary, and it is hard to see how better the holocaust could be remembered, if the dead are to be enshrined with dignity and the warning made endurable.

The sun went down and left its flaxen breath among the pines.

Below, I saw the nestled village of Ain Karem where John the Baptist was born. Over the valley, at the city's farthest reach, was the fine Hadassah Hospital, which keeps a tiny synagogue, its twelve lattices designed over two years by Marc Chagall, who depicted in their glass the tribes of Israel. His child-like world may not evoke them, but he painted a song or a vision – stained glass, he said, is 'something mystical which enters through the window' – and filled his frames with fabulous and airy fragments, crowns and candelabra, the gallop of blue horses in a green night.

The body of Theodor Herzl, the visionary who prophesied Israel's statehood half a century before it came to be, was brought from Vienna in 1949 and buried on the hill on which I stood. He was the founder of political Zionism, who but for his followers would have accepted Uganda as a refuge for the Jews, and never envisaged such suffering as was to come, either to his own people or to others.

'At Basle I founded the Jewish State', he wrote in 1897, after the first Zionist Congress. 'If I said this out loud today I should be greeted by universal laughter. In five years perhaps, and certainly in fifty years, everyone will perceive it.' His grave is a black basalt cube on the windy slope, set where his dream has grown thick on every hill around him. 'If you have the will', he had said, 'it need not be a legend.' Now the terraced glades flow out to farmed valleys, and the hills dip and run under the city's utmost suburbs until they drop away like clouds or curtains.

On the eve of the twentieth anniversary of Israel's independence, twelve torches were lit above Herzl's grave. The streets of West Jerusalem burst into gorges of light where the crowd's heads moved in congested thousands under wide, tinselled discs suspended from the houses, or were swept into dancing to the lilt of accordions. The young spirit of the nation was pulsing through the streets in jeans and Victory hats, natural and exuberant as a new Rome with Hannibal retreated from the gates. Everyone held a plastic hammer which uttered a blink-blink as he hit his neighbour on the head. The strange music had a touch of the East. Fireworks came dancing into the sky to the refrain of the streets, and left their smoke like cobwebs on the stars.

I went back to East Jerusalem. Its battlements were lit, but behind the walls was a profound silence – the Arab city lost in a sleepless gloom – only the lamps' gilding on the lanes, and cats tense and hissing in the dark. Long afterwards, as dawn spread, I could still hear singing outside the walls, and the chatter of the hammers.

The Israeli military parade passed cruelly by the walls of East Jerusalem, and aircraft, flashing and sinister as shark-fins in the sea, left their blue and white trail in broken ribbons over the sky. They came in noiseless swoops or heavy clouds, and sometimes leapt from the close horizon as if a giant were throwing silver knives over Olivet. And a lone Mig. 21 with red-tipped wings soared up from Samaria and vanished like a malignant spirit.

The crowds were quiet as the armour dragged itself upward, and the Patton and French patrol tanks, capped with weathered men, moved by to desultory claps and half-stunned faces. Reconditioned Shermans like armadillos, half-tracks and rocket-launchers, a hundred captured vehicles shaking the earth in growling, lumbering herds, left the air sick with asphalt and the people sated in the weight and noise of caterpillar iron, until the dappled Long Toms passed, which had shelled Tel Aviv, and the march of soldiers lent a half-human touch.

'The soldiers may not look so good,' said a friend in the crowd, a Persian Jew, 'but the world has seen that they are. War is a stimulus to us. Perhaps to the Arabs too. It disrupts the economy but it binds a race and gets quality from it, just as an inquisition finds martyrs. God help us if all this stops!'

He could not tell whether his people would grow into another petty, Levantine nation or would achieve some synthesis of mind and spirit which might bear a new child to civilization. The old Judea had been a country of farmers and warriors; but in dispersion the Jews had adapted to commerce and they were still urban, the flight from the countryside and the *kibbutzim* increasing year by year.

'But the taking of Jerusalem has given us new impetus,' he said. 'When I first walked those old streets I was disgusted. The gap between rich and poor revolted me. But now I love it. I find meanings everywhere. The place is magic.'

He was an oriental Jew of the kind which has found the Arab world familiar and almost comfortable; but he was engaged to an Ashkenaz girl who hated the procession and was bewildered by the Arabs. She was Bulgarian-born, with the heavy-lidded eyes which some subtlety of interbreeding or environment has lent to many western Jews.

'I don't feel anything about Jerusalem. It's as foreign to me as Delhi would be. People keep saying that we have returned. Have we? Where? Is there really a piece of us here? I look at the Wailing Wall and think: are those my people? It's merely a curiosity to me. I am a tourist.'

The difference does not lie simply between the Western and the oriental Jew, for many of the Ashkenazim too have felt a spirit of homecoming. Like most feelings in Jerusalem, it is a ghost out of history. The sense of return is the heritage of the religious, of those who were bound together in the Diaspora by the word of the Torah, by God's promise of a land to His people. In exile the holy book was their country and nation, their morality and law, and filled their lives with a nostalgia for the lost land. As the centuries vanished they saw Jerusalem ideal and immutable. The Roman Empire fell and the Arabs came, Byzantium dying in their wake, and the Crusaders sent a brief flame through Christendom. Two millennia passed. Yet the scattered Jews saw nothing but a waiting land. The feet on her hills were not those of Moslem peasants but the tramp of Judah's warrior-kings and the voice of her prophets. They saw a shining, apocalyptic city, built of the past and the future, but without a present.

'Jerusalem was never prosperous after us, from the Jewish kingdom until now,' the city's mayor told me, and when I disputed this, declared more truly: 'But it was not the centre of a world. The Romans had Rome. The Arabs had Mecca or Damascus. The Turks had Constantinople. Only to us – and perhaps to the Crusaders – has it ever been uniquely important. Now, once again, it is the centre of the world.'

The belief of the Jew in his nation is of its essence religious. To judge it in practical or patriotic terms is to mistake its nature. As in no other race, history has become faith. That part of life which in most countries could be termed secular, is deepened by another dimension, and even the agnostic Jew, born in a free Israel, is conscious of an intense belonging to the Jewish people.

'The Jewish quarter in the Old City will be an enclave of Jews again,' said the mayor. 'This will not be a takeover, just a symbol. It is the symbol which matters – the fact that we have returned.' He was a frank, practical man, tactful with the Arabs and much liked in the Jewish city. He envisaged a future in which the people of Old Jerusalem would find work in factories outside the walls, and the population be thinned and redistributed. The streets would become cleaner and less cluttered, the finer houses restored. Within ten years parks and gardens, following an abandoned British Mandate plan, would be drawn around the walled town and overflow the Kidron valley to Hinnom and the Mount of Olives. Perhaps Jerusalem will then grow closer to the Jewish ideal of the lost city – a dream whose expectations have grown a little sanitary and American over the years, so that the town which Herod knew, whose bazaars overflowed into the Temple, would scarcely be tolerated.

The city and its surroundings are now by Israeli law a part of Israel, and one-fifth of the Old Town has been expropriated. Already changes have come, electricity, water and drainage improved – but its people prefer Arab dirt to Jewish hygiene, and heap a multitude of evils against their new blessings. Some eighty houses were demolished round the Wailing Wall, an area where many North Africans had lived, who traced their descent from the time of Saladin. When the Jews point out their desecrated cemeteries on Olivet, the Arabs murmur about the Mamillah graveyard in West Jerusalem, which has half vanished under a public park. Everything has become more expensive, an taxes, always moderate under Jordan, are crushing. The Israeli government, say the Arabs, gives flamboyantly with one hand and takes away quietly with the other. The Arab hotels are half empty, for the tourist stream has changed its bed and flows not through Amman but through Tel Aviv. Ten thousand new houses will be built round East Jerusalem by 1972, three-quarters of them for Jews, and always there are the whispered rumours of extortion and terrorism.

Jewish taxes, which have given Israel an egalitarian society, are beginning to smooth out the professional classes wealthy under the Arabs. The intelligentsia are leaving for Europe and America, and some of the poor have gone to Amman, where they will probably grow poorer.

'It will take a little time for the Old City to recover financially,' said the mayor. 'But of course we do not expect that prosperity will make people change their wish to be governed by their own kind. The Arabs will always be nationalists – that is their privilege. Such things lie very deep. We can only hope to keep people comfortable. I have great faith in this. So long as they are comfortable, they will not complain. In five hundred years, perhaps, everything will be all right. Meanwhile . . .' he shrugged his heavy shoulders '. . . meanwhile we will await a miracle.'

On any morning by the Damascus Gate one may watch the city, its past and its future, in a handful of passers-by more eloquent than any propaganda. They bear their worlds in their clothes and faces, and seem to relinquish no particle of their heritage in favour of one another: the Orthodox Jew, keeping the pallor of eastern Europe; the priest from Thessaloniki or Athens; the Moslem porter, his legs knotted like olive-trunks, crushed under giant loads; the *sabra*, buoyant and insensitive.

The Jewish and Arab women stare curiously at one another. Two years' military service have formed the Jewish girls capable and graceless. Their clothes and manners are regarded with distaste by conservative Arabs, whose middle-class women dress prettily and have a soft, nurtured look. The difference goes deep between their races, for to the Arabs the senses matter and appearances are in themselves important. But the Israeli, it is said, has lost most of the qualities of the Jew in the Diaspora. He is blunt and forceful, without polish. It is as if a first generation were meeting a last. The sadness penetrates to every layer of being, and the relationship threatens to corrupt both peoples, for the Arab, steeped in centuries of dissimulation under Ottoman misrule, retains his facility to bend and flatter; and the Jew is suspicious and uneasy. The Arabs like the comfort of a large society and grow dispirited when they find themselves few – the meek, in Islam, do not inherit the earth; and the two hundred thousand Jews in the city outnumber them by more than three to one.

There is a widespread feeling of disorientation, as if old weights and measures had been shuffled inextricably together. Surrounded by hostile Arab states, the Jews could not, even if they wished, allow Arabs to reach positions of power in Israel. The more talented will go abroad, and the rest will not develop from the strength of their past – the intangible link which gives a people pride.

No two societies are coupled more poorly. Superiority is inherent in the Jew's heritage. He stands, with his people, in a charmed circle. Amongst them he has always found his strength, and those outside, during two thousand years of persecution, have given him no cause to change. And now, in the land for which his father or his grandfather abandoned everything, whose barren fields he made to flower, he finds a hostility which he feels he has never earned, and subtly believes, perhaps, that the Jew is persecuted again for the ancient sin of being himself.

Yet the Jewish past meant nothing to the Arabs. For thirteen hundred years their ancestors had been dominant in the country – longer than either Christian or Jew – and as they began at last to shake off the stagnation of centuries, another people was imposed upon them as if they were excluded from the natural rights of men. They find with surprise that no voice in the West is raised in their defence. But the damage of the Balfour Declaration, and of centuries of anti-Semitism is already done; and the Arabs are suffering, perhaps, for the conscience of Europe.

For this to prosper, the Holy Land should be peopled by saints; and the days of saints are gone.

13
The Upper Room

As we are all members of Adam
We have heard these melodies in Paradise.
(CELALEDIN RUMI)

I watched the familiar dawn sharpen trees and towers to piercing silhouettes. Not even Jerusalem was yet awake. The paraphernalia which had filled my room for nearly five months had shrunk to a suitcase, standing alone on the cold floor. I looked around to see what I had forgotten, suddenly surprised at the littleness of the cell. There was nothing but its four pieces of furniture, and the picture of an exclamatory saint. I went down the verandah stairs and sat in the courtyard listening to the nuns in their chapel. Jerusalem broke around me in the sparkle of the young sun.

Two of the sisters had walked from the Mount of Olives in the morning darkness to say goodbye, and they all came now to give me presents, standing round the refectory table singing Polish songs of parting in low voices. I lingered foolishly in the courtyard with Gentle Sister, trying to think of something to give her; but I had only bought roses, which were offered back to God in the chapel.

She asked me to pray for the hospice: 'God speaks all languages.'

I stood mumbling gratitude in school German and took her frail, old hand, trying to tell her things confused in my mind. But she said nothing, only gestured in a half farewell, and her eyes filled with watered light, and overflowed.

Laughing Sister giggled and La Grande, looking crumpled and benign, seized me in her arms and kissed the top of my head. The iron door closed behind, and I went into the dawn streets. Madonna walked beside me. Already the markets were stirring as we went south toward the Sion Gate. I shook her hand, which seemed the only way to leave. She stared at me, and turned away while I was still saying goodbye.

★

I walked along the ridge of Sion to the shrine of the Cenacle. The sun was already hard on the Mount of Offence, from whose olive trees the dove of Noah plucked a branch, and brought it as a token to the Ark.

I went on cobbled paths under the tower of the Dormition through buildings which have multiplied like sores on the aging trunk of the Cenacle. Hadrian, wrote Bishop Epiphanius in the fourth century, had found Jerusalem in ruins except for a few houses and a little church from which 'the disciples had gone up to the Cenacle', the room of the Last Supper. The Byzantines built their church of Haghia Sion splendidly beside it, and the tradition remained in Crusader and Franciscan restorations and the records of early travellers. Here Christ – so sixteen hundred years of Christendom believed – gave his flesh and blood in symbol to the world, a sacrifice of life for the renewal of man's spirit, and washed the feet of his disciples before they went down to Gethsemane in the full moon of Passover. And here the disciples were sitting at Pentecost when the Holy Spirit descended in a tempest, 'and there appeared unto them cloven tongues like as of fire, and it sat upon each of them' (Acts 2:3).

I went through a medieval doorway and up stairs high through the clutter of walls and plastered Islamic domes. The room was beautifully proportioned, the vaults flowing up from ancient pillars, graceful and sure. But this was no dark, subtle closet for oriental intimacies, the cushioned closeness of a last farewell, but had been built by craftsmen whom the Franciscans had brought from Cyprus six hundred years before. An ambitious, Western majesty struck upward in its sheaf of vaults: a Gothic hall for the clash of goblets and the gauntness of bone-tearing Crusader hounds, for drunken lute-players and women's peep-holes. Even the site, in the new light of archaeology, can scarcely be that of the Last Supper, and in medieval times – a token of the unreliability of tradition – the 'Tomb of David' was located here on a misreading of the Bible.

A Crusader chronicler found the 'tomb' already established with those of Solomon and St Stephen, and at other times the chalice of the Last Supper could be seen, with the Holy Lance, the Crown of Thorns, and the stones which killed St Stephen. In the fifteenth century the Moslems, who venerate David, took the building from the Franciscans, set a *mihrab* in the Upper Room and refused access to all but those of their own faith.

I descended to the tomb under a columned cupola across whose capitals owls linked their marble wings, and wandered by Crusader rooms, cloistered and empty, where pilgrims' candle-grease hung in frosty spears from every wall. To the east the graves of the Moslem Da'udneh – the keepers of the tomb of David – lay forgotten in the glow of Byzantine stones which had once borne up the lovely Haghia Sion. But the tomb itself was in darkness – a Cyclopean, elongated mound, like the graves of those mythic heroes which scatter the Lebanese hills – filling the length of its narrow chamber and covered by a wine-red cloth on which the lions of Judah danced. The Moslems, fanatic guardians for close on five hundred years, have lost the tomb to the Jews, but they still venerate it from afar and their *mihrab*, with its flower-patterned tiles, points faithfully to Mecca.

The Jews have set the grave with silver crowns – one for each year of Israel's new statehood – which glitter in a cloud of candles. Beneath, they say, is a cave where David lies, 'a sovereign prince in the earth', and haunts the tomb, when all are gone, in robes of glistening lead. Peasants of the three religions pray for his intercession, and fear that if they break their vows they will go blind and their cattle die. Barren women plead fertility, for David's line continued twenty-two generations, and the Jews, in the prayer of blessing the moon, still claim that 'David, king of Israel, is alive and active'.

A pair of rabbis stood by the cenotaph.

A bashful young man approached for a blessing on his mother.

'She is living?' demanded a rabbi.

'Yes,' he whispered. 'Still.'

'What's her name?'

'Hannah.'

The rabbi incanted for a few seconds, words harsh and formular, while another thrust forward the offertory. The flame on the blackened walls, the prayer of priests, the murmurs and shufflings were any echo of the past. The sects have come and gone, but the tribal sense remains, the certainties and loves of those who know.

The tomb remembers all three faiths. It might have been a forum for their unity, but became instead a focus of scheming and narrowness since medieval years. The closer drew their beliefs, the angrier they became with one another, the more rigid their tenure of the shrine.

But reason and human tenderness have stripped bigotry of its virtue, and only the simple believe that the monument stands above the grave of the shepherd-king, or dogma over age-long truths. Jerusalem, where half the world's religion grew – the shining concept of the personal God – is already changing. The young Jew rejects the Law of his people, and nationalism, not Islam, is the heart of Arab brotherhood. The eastern music falters. The tremor of the future is upon it – the thrust of science, the dependence of the world upon itself. Again men have enquired into their beliefs and many have found only themselves, a reflection of psychoses and desires. Perhaps people deserve the gods they find, their Avengers and Comforters and Absolutes. 'The soul,' said Plato, 'divines that which it seeks.' As the Franciscans saw the Upper Room in a Gothic hall, so the image of God may be textured to people's minds. Divinity, says the Hasid, is like an ocean which can be poured into many cups, and only the shape of a man's soul restricts it.

The Jewish sages saw the Last Day as the justification of a nation. The world would be pierced by tunnels through which the dead would roll to Jerusalem, where a bridge of iron and a bridge of paper would offer all mankind a passage to the feet of God on Olivet. The unbelievers, choosing the bridge of iron, would vanish from sight, while the Children of Israel passed to their heritage on the bridge of paper. The measurements of the New Jerusalem were given with exactitude by Ezekiel. They were not large enough to hold a very generous portion of humanity, and although the Dead Sea Scrolls speak of a greater town, with twelve towered gates, it was, in essence, the heaven of a single people.

The Moslems, in their catholic fashion, have a legend that Christ will judge the departed. Those who cried unbelieving, 'When we are dead, transformed to dust and bones, can we be raised to life with those before us?' will squirm in hot winds and smoke, while the rest will ascend to a paradise heady with fruit and rivers and 'dark-eyed houris chaste as hidden pearls' (Koran 56), a sensuous but righteous Eden with masculine delights.

Thus God for a time is close and ready – 'As the mountains are round about Jerusalem, so the Lord is round about his people' – until the mind awakes to other vistas. Then the gardens and paper bridges begin to wither, and are counted as symbols before these too become outworn. The mystics reach for their communion in the incense-dream of the Greek Orthodox, the ecstasy of the Hasid or the dance of the Sufi. Whatever he may imagine, man's essence is religious, and passion and humility – the gifts of Judea – seem vital to the balance in his soul. Jerusalem is still the spirit-city, a ghost-name for the yearnings of the world. Men fight for her as Greeks and Trojans over the body of Patroclus, not for what she is but for what she represents.

'We have an everlasting city', wrote St Paul, 'but not here; our goal is the city that is one day to be.' This vision grants all movement, all purpose, for without the horizon the traveller despairs. It tints with hope the worldly kingdom, whose disinherited children may see it hanging mystically in the sky, as they did long ago in Judea – suspended, they cannot tell, by the hand of God or the eye of man – and let it illumine as it may the earthly city, vigorous and precious in its light.

Select Bibliography

P. B. BAGATTI, OFM, *Scavo di un Monastero al 'Dominus Flevit'*, Liber Annus VI, Studii Biblici Franciscani, 1955–6.

P. B. BAGATTI, OFM, *Scoperta di un Cimitero Guideo-Cristiano al 'Dominus Flevit'*, Liber Annus III, Studii Biblici Franciscani, 1953.

P. B. BAGATTI, OFM, and J. T. MILIK, *Gli Scavi del 'Dominus Flevit'*, Pubblicazioni dello Studium Biblicum Franciscanum, 1958.

G. K. CHESTERTON, *The New Jerusalem*, Hodder & Stoughton, London, 1920.

K. A. C. CRESWELL, *Early Muslim Architecture*, 2 vols, Clarendon Press, Oxford, 1932, 1940.

J. W. CROWFOOT, *Early Churches in Palestine*, British Academy, 1941.

ARCHDEACON DOWLING, *The Abyssinian Church*, Cope, Fenwick, London, 1910.

ARCHDEACON DOWLING, *The Patriarchate of Jerusalem*, SPCK, London, 1909.

ALFRED EDERSHEIM, *The Temple: its ministry and service*, Pickering & Inglis, London, 1958.

HARRY EMERSON FOSDICK, *A Pilgrimage to Palestine*, SCM, London, 1928.

GEORGE JEFFERY, *The Holy Sepulchre*, CUP, Cambridge, 1919.

C. N. JOHNS, *The Citadel of Jerusalem, A Summary of work since 1934*, Quarterly of the Department of Antiquities in Palestine, XIV, 1950.

C. N. JOHNS, *Guide to the Citadel of Jerusalem*, Gov. Palestine Department of Antiquities, 1944.

MICHEL JOIN-LAMBERT, *Jerusalem*, Trs. Charlotte Haldane, Elek Books, London, 1958.

FLAVIUS JOSEPHUS, *Complete Works*, Trs. William Whiston, Pickering & Inglis, London, 1960.

KATHLEEN M. KENYON. *Jerusalem. Excavating 3000 Years of History*,

Thames & Hudson, London, 1967.

GUY LE STRANGE, *Palestine under the Moslems*, Translated from the works of the mediaeval Arabian geographers, Palestine Exploration Fund, 1890.

BEATRICE LEVERTOFF, *Jerusalem in the time of Christ*, National Soc. & SPCK, London, 1945.

D. S. MARGOLIOUTH, *Cairo, Jerusalem and Damascus*, Chatto & Windus, London, 1907.

SOEUR MARIE ALINE DE SION, *La Forteresse Antonia à Jérusalem et la question du Pretoire*, Franciscan Press, Jerusalem, 1955.

CHARLES D. MATTHEWS, *Palestine – Mohammedan Holy Land*, Yale University Press, 1949.

ELINOR A. MOORE, *The Ancient Churches of Old Jerusalem*, Constable & Co., London, 1961.

W. D. MORRISON, *The Jews under Roman Rule*. T. Fisher Unwin, London, 1885.

H. V. MORTON, *In the Steps of the Master*, Methuen and Co., London, 1937.

W. O. E. OESTERLEY, *The Jews and Judaism during the Greek Period*, SPCK, London, 1941.

A. PARROT, *Golgotha et Saint-Sepulchre*, Neuchâtel, 1955.

A. PARROT, *Le Temple de Jérusalem*, Neuchâtel, 1955.

STEWART PEROWNE, *In Jerusalem and Bethlehem*, Hodder & Stoughton, London, 1964.

STEWART PEROWNE, *The Life and Times of Herod the Great*, Hodder & Stoughton, London, 1956.

STEWART PEROWNE, *The One Remains*, Hodder & Stoughton, London, 1954.

ERMETE PIEROTTI, *Jerusalem Explored*, Trs. Thomas Bonney, Bell & Daldy, London, 1864.

E. T. RICHMOND, *The Dome of the Rock in Jerusalem*, Clarendon Press, Oxford, 1924.

REINHOLD RÖHRICHT, *Bibliotheca Geographica Palaestinae*, H. Reuther's Verlagsbuchhandlung, 1890.

STEVEN RUNCIMAN, *A History of the Crusades*, 3 vols, CUP, Cambridge, 1953–4.

HENRI SAUVAIRE, *Histoire de Jérusalem et d'Hébron*, Fragments de la Chronique de Moudjir-ed-din, Ernest Leroux, 1876.

J. SIMONS, *Jerusalem in the Old Testament*, E. J. Brill, Leiden, 1952.

JALALU'D-DIN AS-SUYUTI, *History of the Temple of Jerusalem*, Oriental Translation Fund, 1836.

PETER THOMSEN, *Die Palastina-Literatur*, Akademie-Verlag, Berlin, 1960.

ZEV VILNAY, *Legends of Palestine*, The Jewish Publication Society of America, 1932.

L.-HUGUES VINCENT, *Jérusalem Antique*, Librairie Victor Lecoffre, Paris, 1912.

L.-HUGUES VINCENT, *Underground Jerusalem*, Horace Cox, London, 1911.

L.-HUGUES VINCENT and F. M. ABEL, *Jérusalem Nouvelle*, 4 vols, Librairie Victor Lecoffre, Paris, 1914–26.

L.-HUGUES VINCENT and P. M.-A. STEVE, *Jérusalem de l'Ancien Testament*, 2 vols, Librairie Victor Lecoffre, Paris, 1954–6.

MELCHOIR DE VOGUÉ, *Le Temple de Jérusalem*, Paris, 1864.

CPTS. WILSON & WARREN, *The Recovery of Jerusalem*, Richard Bentley & Sons, London, 1871.

Index

Though the abbreviation 'St' is used, saints, as well as the churches dedicated to them, are to be found indexed under 'Saint'.